THE MISUNDERSTOOD HIGHLY SENSITIVE PERSON

A GUIDE FOR HSPS TO THRIVE IN AN INSENSITIVE WORLD

SALLY ANN

CONTENTS

INTRODUCTION

Sensitivity is a sign of strength. It's not about toughening up, it's about smartening up.

— MARIE FORLEO

Has anyone ever told you that you were "too sensitive?" Have you ever felt like you react more strongly to certain situations than others would? Do you find that you have to remove yourself from certain situations in order to recover emotionally? Then when you try to tell people about it, they just tell you to "toughen up" or have a "stiff upper lip"? All your life it's like you've been misunderstood and unheard about this part of yourself.

Things seem to get to you more easily and strike at your emotional core. You might feel, through all these things, that you have the world's volume turned up higher than everyone else does and you wonder if you're the only one who feels this way.

Well, you're not alone. Even if it might not seem like it, there are millions of people just like you who deal with these very same feelings every day. People who live just like you: avoiding certain intense situations or reacting "too strongly" to stimulating things. These people are known as highly sensitive people. If you connect to any of the questions above or have ever wondered if you're a little too sensitive, you might belong to this community.

HSPs, as they are known, form a strong community. Many of them have found that identifying their sensitivity has helped them connect with others and better understand themselves and their lives. They have also found that sharing their experiences with one another has helped them build coping mechanisms and develop strategies for dealing with their sensitivity in an insensitive world. There are also lots of them: It is estimated that around 15–20% of people are highly sensitive (*Being "Highly Sensitive,"* 2018). Though they might be quiet, HSPs are everywhere.

It's also important to know that being an HSP is not a bad thing! Highly sensitive people might experience certain difficulties, but most live rich and fulfilling lives, especially if they have identified some key coping mechanisms and constructed a strong support system. Many HSPs also use their sensitive qualities to their advantage by pursuing careers that help others or helping build communities. Even if you identify yourself as an HSP, you can still reach your full potential and live your best life.

You probably feel like your sensitivity is controlling your life and like you can't do all the things you want to do because you are sensitive. Maybe there have been job offers you've turned down because they meant moving to a bigger city. Perhaps you've avoided parties or festivals because crowds are too stressful for you. Receiving party invitations may not be your ultimate goal, but you want to have the power to choose whether or not you go without your sensitivity automatically precluding you. In short, you want to take back control of your life and find a way to manage your sensitivity in a way that is more than just "toughening up."

If you're reading this book, you may have struggled with some of these things before. You're confused about why you always feel so deeply affected and overwhelmed by things and want a way to better your situation. You're frustrated by our world which values toughness so much and leaves so little room to be sensitive or vulnerable. You're sick of people telling you that you just need to "calm down" or "push through" because they don't seem to have dealt with the same things you have. Well, you've come to the right place. In this book, we will outline the experience of a highly sensitive person and share some key insights into the ins and outs of the HSP experience. We will also provide some important tips and coping mechanisms for managing your emotions and creating strong support systems so you can properly deal with your anxieties when they arise.

In the life you imagine for yourself, you're probably happy and free. Your sensitivity isn't necessarily gone, but you have it more under your control and aren't defined by it. You can maybe advance a little further outside your comfort zone using some of your new coping mechanisms and can better read your emotions to know when to take a break or remove yourself from a situation. You want to be able to live without fear and without feeling like you can't do all the things you want to do. Hopefully, in this book, you will find some important tools to help you work toward the kind of life you envision for yourself.

Chapters 1–3 will focus on the highly sensitive person's life and feelings. What you will find in the first few chapters is a reflection of your experiences, helping you identify what behaviors of yours might pertain to a highly sensitive personality. These early chapters will examine the daily realities of living with high sensitivity and help you learn about what makes you feel this way. At the end of these chapters, you should be able to relatively accurately identify whether the highly sensitive person label describes you or someone you know.

Chapters 4–6 then pivot to solutions and coping mechanisms for people with high sensitivity. They will guide you through some strategies for managing your emotions during high-stress situations. They will also provide you guidance on how to communicate your feelings to others and set strong boundaries for your needs. These middle chapters will start to unpack the HSP experience and help guide you toward overcoming these fears.

The last section of the book will end on a high note, looking at some of the benefits of high sensitivity. This section will also offer a change in perspective, shifting to the point of view of an HSP supporter. This section is a great resource to provide to friends and family if you are an HSP and to learn things yourself if you are close to an HSP or even a parent of one. Being surrounded by understanding people is one of the most important parts of the HSP toolkit.

Through all of this book's sections, we will discuss why you feel the way you do, how those feelings manifest, and how they limit your life, then we will offer you some strategies and solutions to help you break these patterns and learn to take care of yourself and your feelings. By the end of this book, you'll be an expert on your own sensitivity and have the ability to articulate your feelings and manage them so that you can live the free and healthy lifestyle you deserve!

1

THE WORLD OF HIGH SENSITIVITY

We live in a stimulating world, but for some, that stimulation is felt more intensely. For highly sensitive people, things that might seem ordinary can be very difficult. Things like bright lighting, loud environments, clothing tags, or even certain fabrics can be very distracting to someone who is highly sensitive. In this chapter, we will look at the signs of high sensitivity in order for you to identify whether your behaviors qualify as highly sensitive.

One important disclaimer to note is that "highly sensitive" is not a diagnosis. There is no official designation or diagnostic criteria for being an HSP, and it is not listed as a mental disorder. HSP is a descriptive title that provides a way for you to identify with others through shared experiences, not a medical problem.

You can think of these criteria as more of a checklist for identifying a personality type or an attachment style. It is important to identify yourself in order to be able to look into solutions, but you don't need to seek medical attention unless you exhibit symptoms of another officially-designated mental disorder. In other words, identifying as an HSP does not need to be signed off by a doctor and is just a tool for you to understand yourself and help improve your life.

WHAT IS A HIGHLY SENSITIVE PERSON?

A highly sensitive person is generally defined as anyone who has an above-average emotional reaction to certain stimuli. As an HSP, you will find that situations that seem normal to others will elicit a strong reaction from you. For example, even though going to concerts is a common and popular pastime, they may cause you extreme emotional distress, or maybe you notice that your friends can wear clothing with tags on the back of the neck, but you obsessively cut yours out to avoid extreme discomfort. Highly sensitive people tend to often notice that their experience is markedly different from those of their friends and family, leading them to wonder if there's something wrong with them.

There is also considerable crossover with other conditions and high sensitivity. You might find that there are other symptom lists you strongly relate to with the exception of just a few of the symptoms. Anxiety disorders have perhaps the most crossover since high sensitivity can cause anxiety. You might have even been diagnosed with and treated for an anxiety disorder. Similarly, if you experience high sensitivity, you might have some things in common with those on the autism spectrum, but you may not exhibit other symptoms. So, high sensitivity can both be a symptom of a larger problem or a condition on its own.

CHARACTERISTICS OF A HIGHLY SENSITIVE PERSON

Not all highly sensitive people are the same; most have particular things that cause them distress. Where one highly sensitive person might be completely fine in a certain situation, another might be at their wit's end. Some people are more sensitive to sounds, some more to emotions, some more to light, and so on. It is important, then, to examine all aspects of your life when thinking about your relationship to high sensitivity. In this section, we will list some of the main characteristics shared by highly sensitive people and give clear examples of these characteristics by relating them to real-life situations. When reading this section, try to picture yourself in some of these situations and reflect on what your reaction might be. By learning about different facets of high sensitivity, you will be able to better understand how high sensitivity manifests for you in particular and develop a clearer understanding of yourself and your emotions.

Processing Environmental Stimuli More Deeply

Perhaps the trademark trait of a highly sensitive person, extreme reactions to your environment are a telltale sign you might be an HSP. You find that being in overstimulating environments will cause you great distress and discomfort. You might respond by freezing up, having a panic attack, becoming irritable, or even needing to remove yourself. Even though you might see that everyone around you is having a good time, all these reactions are normal if you consider the degree to which you feel affected. There's no reason to be ashamed of any of these reactions.

We have already given some fairly obvious examples of very clearly overstimulating environments that even non-highly sensitive people might find overstimulating including parties, concerts, and big cities. Other examples of places that might elicit similar reactions in highly sensitive people are malls, schools (especially cafeterias or assemblies), movie theaters, and even museums. All these environments share a few common traits: crowds, open spaces, loud noises, and bright or flashing lights. Generally, these are the primary kinds of environmental stimuli that highly sensitive people react to.

However, these are mostly just lights and noise. What about some other environments that might be stimulating in other ways? Any environment that causes you to hide your emotional state, remain standing for a long period of time, or any of the other multitude of uncomfortable things that can be just as overstimulating to an HSP as the mosh pit at a metal concert. You might find that, for you, the worst places are actually things like family dinners, your work environment (especially if you are in customer service), or airplanes, among other similar things. The environment doesn't always matter: You can experience high sensitivity anywhere.

Behavioral Inhibition

Another side to the highly sensitive person is an aversion to novelty, also known as "behavioral inhibition." If you notice yourself sticking to the same routine, it might be because of high sensitivity. This may look like eating the same foods every day, going to the same cafe every morning, or having certain clothing items or TV shows that you feel like you must wear or watch. Highly sensitive people might dislike things like travel, which is all about putting yourself in an unfamiliar environment where you don't know what your experiences are going to be. While most people find novelty exciting, HSPs see it as dangerous. Familiarity is a friend of a highly sensitive person.

Highly sensitive people experience extreme distress in uncomfortable situations, so they greatly fear the unknown since they have no idea if they are going to be launched into the kind of extreme distress they are prone to. There are so many situations where HSPs can feel very afraid, so they try their best to limit their exposure to potentially overstimulating phenomena. There is probably a list of things that you know over-stimulate you, but what about the things you haven't tried yet? For those HSPs who have been let down before, trying something new can be much scarier than it is for the average person.

Strong Unconscious Nervous System Activity

A classic anxiety symptom is increased activity of your unconscious nervous system, which means that your vitals are working at a higher speed than normal. This could be your heartbeat, but it can also be breathing and swallowing. These responses are your body's way of dealing with anxiety. It all relates to evolutionary sources where stress was usually due to being chased by a beast or a fire. By increasing your heart rate and causing you to breathe faster, your body is giving you the energy to run away fast. Since you likely won't need this extra running energy in a crowded movie theater in the 21st century, these symptoms can be disruptive. If you notice these symptoms in highly stimulating environments, you might be experiencing some sensitivity.

Having Stronger Emotional Responses

It's not just loud noises that can cause highly sensitive people distress; emotions can do this, too. In addition to being sensitive to intense environmental stimuli, HSPs tend to report stronger emotional responses to things like others' pain, intense conversations, and even movies or books. HSPs often score very highly in empathy, and many become psychologists or counselors. From this perspective, emotional sensitivity can be a good thing. However, it can also be very emotionally taxing for those who experience it and can cause extreme distress. Perhaps you cannot help crying during most movies or are very upset by your friend telling you about a traumatic experience. While these reactions can be normal, a highly sensitive person might react much more strongly or even obsess about these things for days on end. So, the heightened emotional state of the highly sensitive person can be both their greatest weakness and greatest strength.

Being Intensely Aware of Subtle Differences

Highly sensitive people might also have keen eyes as well. Because they interpret their environment so intensely, everything seems much bigger. Imagine it's like they're putting up a magnifying glass to the world and everything is hyper-exaggerated. For this reason, highly sensitive people often notice things that others don't like distant music playing or even a carefully hidden mood on someone's face. Again, as with emotional sensitivity, this can be both a blessing and a curse. While HSPs can make great writers and detectives because they pick up on subtleties that others don't, it can also be very distracting and overwhelming to be constantly focusing on tiny details. Consider this quote by George Eliot from his book *Middlemarch* (*Middlemarch quotes*, n.d.):

If we had a keen vision and feeling of all ordinary human life, it would be like hearing the grass grow and the squirrel's heart beat, and we should die of that roar which lies on the other side of silence.

The author, a woman writing under a male pseudonym, is saying that even though we might think we'd like to know everything about the universe, to hear every little thing would actually be like hearing a great roar and would be too overstimulating to handle. This quote quite clearly sums up the experience of a hypersensitive person: hearing things that others might not notice and becoming intensely overwhelmed.

Having Low Sensory Output Tolerance

Highly sensitive people don't just have trouble taking in information; they may also struggle with putting it out as well. Conversations are often very taxing for an HSP because they are forced to both receive and send stimuli. HSPs who struggle with sensory output might find that things like public speaking, writing, or telling a long story can be excessively draining. Their intense sensitivity requires them to put a lot of care into these things and therefore possibly exert more energy than the average person. Often HSPs, especially those who are introverted, will need long periods for recharging in between social gatherings as talking is one of the most overstimulating activities for them.

Having a Low Pain Threshold

More seriously, highly sensitive people might actually respond to pain more strongly than others. Even a minor injury like stubbing your toe might be extremely upsetting for a highly sensitive person. For this reason, HSPs often avoid risky situations; some are even afraid of becoming pregnant because of the extreme physical pain and discomfort involved. They've probably been told that they were overreacting to certain injuries, but for those with high sensitivity, it is very real.

SIGNS YOU MIGHT BE A HIGHLY SENSITIVE PERSON

Now that you know the general characteristics of highly sensitive people, we will list some of the less obvious signs that you might have some high sensitivity. These are things that many people do, but highly sensitive people tend to do them more or feel them more deeply. If you find yourself relating to most of these things, you might be a highly sensitive person.

You Have Been Told You're Emotional

You've heard it all before: You're taking things too hard or you take longer than the average person to get over things. Maybe it took you two years to get over your six-month relationship, maybe you cry if someone makes a joke about you, or maybe you even get extremely frustrated over a store being out of your favorite brand. These are just examples, but they illustrate how HSPs will often feel things more deeply or take longer to process things than other individuals, even something most would perceive as simply a minor inconvenience. Others might not understand this and call you emotional, but you know that what you're feeling is real.

You're Very Compassionate

One of the best things about HSPs is their compassion. They will be able to connect with others and pick up on their emotions very easily. If you tend to be a go-to person for others to talk about their pain or struggles, you might be a highly sensitive person. The problem is that empathizing with others can be extremely draining to HSPs, causing you to perhaps have a love-hate relationship with counseling your friends through their issues. This trait might also lead you to have extreme reactions to violence or cruelty. Many HSPs become activists because of this sensitivity, channeling their empathy into practical justice work.

You Overthink

Another crossover with anxiety is that highly sensitive people often overthink and obsess about seemingly inconsequential things. You might spend hours dwelling over whether something you said to your friend was rude or offensive, or not be able to sleep after events like job interviews or auditions. Highly sensitive people are very concerned about what others think and experience constant worry over their behavior.

Deadlines Are Very Stressful for You

School and work deadlines tend to be the kryptonite of many HSPs. Because of a high drive to impress and implicit perfectionism, many HSPs find deadlines to be extremely stressful. It is best for HSPs to be in jobs that do not require this kind of pressure and to find work that helps them thrive without stress.

You're Intuitive

Have you ever felt like you could guess what someone was going to say before they said it or felt like you knew something was wrong with someone before they told you? HSPs are often able to pick up on extremely subtle social cues, even being able to surmise things about people that they didn't even know themselves. If you have sometimes thought you were psychic, you might actually just be highly sensitive.

You're Easily Startled

Highly sensitive people often respond very strongly to sudden movements or jumpscares. This is why many find horror movies to be extremely distressing and try to avoid them altogether.

You Can Be Irritable

Highly sensitive people are often uncomfortable. They are almost always in a situation that is at least a little bit overstimulating in some way, so they are usually dealing with some level of distress. Thus, it can be hard for them to control their emotions, and they can become testy with other people. However, if you learn to manage your stimuli, this irritability should subside.

You're Very Easily Tired

No one likes to be the first to leave a party, but for HSPs, it's sometimes inevitable. You feel like your battery life is much shorter than that of those around you and often will be the first to leave or stop an activity. This might cause some annoyance among your friends, but those who understand your feelings will be happy to let you go and recharge somewhere safe and comfortable.

You Avoid Conflict

Perhaps one of the most debilitating traits of the highly sensitive person is conflict avoidance. Conflict is a necessary part of life, but it is also very distressing. This is especially true for those HSPs who are very emotionally sensitive and have trouble handling criticism. This avoidance of conflict can actually lead to a multitude of issues including not wanting to speak up in meetings or classes and staying in unhealthy relationships.

You Have a Rich Inner World

Highly sensitive people tend to be very deep thinkers. Just as their outside world is very overstimulating, their minds tend to be overstimulating as well. Perhaps you are constantly meditating on philosophical concepts, or political issues, or even writing stories in your head, or maybe having imaginary conversations with people. This can be the perfect mindset for a creative person or an academic. However, HSPs can actually suffer from things like insomnia because of this inability to "turn off" their brains. Again, like many of the other qualities of the highly sensitive person, this one is both a perk and a burden.

THE CAUSES OF HIGH SENSITIVITY

The roots of high sensitivity are different for everyone and can be unique to each highly sensitive person. However, there are some common roots we can trace high sensitivity back to. In this section, we will look at some of the typical causes of high sensitivity, helping you consider where your feelings might have come from.

Evolution

As we talked about before, there are certain evolutionary survival reasons for people to be highly sensitive. Being acutely aware of your environment has immense benefits when trying to be wary of predators. Perhaps there is a gene that designates certain people as biological watch people, those who are more apt to sense threats than others. Of course, these skills are not as applicable in our modern world and frequently come into conflict with contemporary life.

Environment

Depending on where you live and where you're from, you may have been exposed to an environment that required you to be highly sensitive. Maybe you grew up in a rural environment where there were very few stimuli then moved to a more populated area where you are constantly surrounded by noise. This would make anyone feel overwhelmed, and some people never recover from the shift. Drastically changing your environment can create high sensitivity that is essentially your body trying to cope with the intense changes it is experiencing.

Genetics

Some people might just be predisposed to highly sensitive feelings. Like many other traits, such as left-handedness, scientists just don't know whether this quality is genetic or why. It is not clear whether these qualities run in families or how much the environment plays a role, but there is a strong likelihood that genetics are relevant as well.

Trauma

Many people who have had traumatic experiences, such as childhood trauma, report experiencing high sensitivity later in life. This usually develops out of necessity. For example, if someone had an abusive parent that forced them to constantly walk on eggshells, they might never feel like they can truly express themselves or set boundaries. Sometimes, high sensitivity is actually a trauma response.

Connection With Other Conditions

As we've mentioned, there is often crossover between high sensitivity and other conditions such as autism spectrum disorder, anxiety, ADHD, OCD, and others. If you experience high sensitivity, you should also look into some of these other things as high sensitivity can be a symptom of something larger. It can exist on its own as well, but those who have been diagnosed with another mental illness or disorder might connect this to their high sensitivity.

MOVING FORWARD

From this chapter, you've hopefully gotten a better idea of how high sensitivity might fit into your own life. You may have found that something you thought was completely normal is in fact something that only highly sensitive people experience. Maybe you even discovered that what you thought was anxiety is actually better described as high sensitivity. In the next chapter, we will dive deeper into some of the real-world experiences of HSPs and look at some of their strengths as well as some of the challenges they face.

2

THE UPS AND DOWNS OF THE HIGHLY SENSITIVE

You cannot make everyone think and feel as deeply as you do. This is your tragedy, because you understand them but they do not understand you.

— DANIEL SAINT

The life of a highly sensitive person is not like the lives of others. This is not to say that they necessarily have worse lives but merely that they have distinctly different experiences. In this chapter, we will look at how highly sensitive traits manifest in real-world situations and how they can affect the lives of those living with high sensitivity.

CHALLENGES OF THE HIGHLY SENSITIVE PERSON

Life with high sensitivity can have its learning curves. There are many ways in which our world is unforgiving to high sensitivity. We live in a world full of loud, abrasive noises and glaring lights, a world where you can feel left out if you don't participate when these things are present. Having certain environments that trigger you and things you can't participate in can make you feel like a social pariah, but there's no need to feel this way. Your needs are valid, and with the right accommodations, there's no reason they can't be met. Here, we will look at some of the challenges an HSP might face in our world today.

Easily Overwhelmed

One of the most common struggles highly sensitive people face is constantly feeling overwhelmed. They often feel like the world is too much for them, that sounds are too loud, lights are too bright, or rooms are too crowded. Sometimes everyday tasks or situations can be extremely daunting for a highly sensitive person. For example, most people think going to the grocery store is no big deal, but for certain highly sensitive people, the task fills them with anxiety. The chaotic parking lot, the massive building, the crowds of people, and the multitude of products can set off a highly sensitive person's anxieties very easily.

As mentioned before, there are different triggers for becoming overwhelmed. Some people find that emotional situations wear them out more than environmental stimulation. Because of the HSP's deeply caring nature, they tend to feel emotional situations more intensely than others, causing them to feel overwhelmed more easily. Hearing someone describe a traumatic experience or seeing someone be humiliated is difficult for most people, but for a highly sensitive person, it can be completely devastating. They might have to remove themselves from a situation or avoid situations or media where there are intense emotional experiences. This tendency to be easily overwhelmed is one of the most debilitating aspects of being an HSP.

Social Anxiety

Along the same lines as emotional sensitivity, some highly sensitive people find social interactions to be very daunting. This is true even when these social interactions are superficial or have lower stakes, such as small talk. In fact, this early getting-to-know-you stage of relationships can be one of the most difficult and painful parts of human interaction for an HSP. Because their high sensitivity causes them to intensely fear rejection, many HSPs avoid pursuing new relationships. This is a shame because HSPs make great friends, so letting fear of ridicule or rejection hold them back means that lots of us miss out on getting to know some amazing people.

In more extreme cases, this social anxiety can move into a fear of intimacy. Close relationships create a whole other set of anxieties for an HSP. These anxieties revolve around being seen in a more intimate way and the emotional taxation of deep connections. Though the fear of rejection is lessened, the depth of feeling expressed in a closer relationship can be equally over-whelming for an HSP. This can sometimes cause them to occasionally retreat from people to whom they are close in order to recharge from the emotional intensity. This can cause strain on their relationships and do real harm to their ability to maintain close connections in their life.

Difficulty Setting Boundaries

One of the most debilitating aspects of a highly sensitive person's life is their difficulty with saying no to people. Because of their intense awareness of others' feelings, they tend to feel immense guilt when they let anyone down. In some ways, this can be a good thing. HSPs almost always follow through with their commitments and are hardly ever flaky, especially when someone might get hurt as a result of their negligence.

If you have an HSP on your team, you can be sure that they will come through for you and make sure they do their part. So, this difficulty with setting boundaries can, in some ways, lead to a strong commitment on the part of the HSP.

However, on the other hand, HSPs might find themselves becoming doormats or people pleasers because it is simply too painful for them to experience letting someone down. They might find themselves taking on too much work at their job or committing to too many volunteer opportunities simply because they were asked. They risk putting their physical and mental health on the line by spreading themselves too thin. In the worst cases, people who like to take advantage of others might manipulate the HSP's lack of boundaries and exploit their agreeability for their own personal gain. In order to avoid this, HSPs must learn to assuage their guilt around saying no to people and set boundaries.

The lack of boundary-setting among HSPs can become especially dangerous when it comes to their emotional life. While their lack of boundaries at work might cause them to burn out, their lack of emotional boundaries can leave them vulnerable to manipulation. HSPs listen closely to the pain and struggles of others and share in those feelings very deeply, so they often become emotional crutches or unpaid therapists to many people in their lives. In more serious cases, they can also end up being victims of emotional manipulation by narcissists or inconsiderate people. This side of the importance of setting boundaries is very important for HSPs to establish since their emotional well-being and safety in relationships are at stake.

"Failure to Launch" Syndrome

One danger of highly sensitive personalities, especially in teenagers and young adults, is that their extreme sense of comfort in their current life can cause them to fear entering the adult world. Thus, a common predicament among some HSPs is what is called "failure to launch" syndrome, which refers to an inability to "launch" from the adolescent world into the adult world. This might mean struggling with moving out on their own, preferring the comforting security of their childhood home. It might also mean struggling to hold down a full-time job because the stress of working is too much for them. They might also struggle to reach adult milestones, such as getting into romantic relationships. Anything associated with moving on from childhood can cause certain HSPs to spiral into anxiety; the fear of leaving their old life behind and venturing out into completely foreign territory is too overwhelming for them.

This syndrome can cause great strain on an HSP's life and the lives of those around them. Failure to launch can limit HSPs professionally and cause them difficulties in pursuing a career. It can also stunt their personal development, leaving them far behind their peers with platonic and romantic relationships to the point where they might become social outcasts. The older you get, the harder it may become to explain on first dates that you've never been in a relationship—or maybe never even been kissed. Of course, everyone goes about life at their own speed, but those experiencing failure to launch are actively limiting themselves in their pursuit of an adult life due to of fear. Relating back to the discussion in Chapter 1 about HSPs loving comfort, the inability to move into the adult world is an example of just that.

Failure to launch is also stressful for the HSP's loved ones, especially parents or caregivers. For HSPs who are still living at home, parents might feel at a loss for how to help their children grow and move on with their lives. On one hand, they don't want to hurt their child or make them feel unwanted by kicking them out of the house, but on the other hand, they don't want to be enablers who allow their child to keep wallowing in fear and never truly living. For all those involved, failure to launch can be extremely stressful and is one of the most harmful patterns HSPs might fall into.

Difficulty With Change

Along the same lines, HSPs often struggle with changes in their life. This might not be as extreme as a failure-to-launch situation and can happen at any age to varying degrees. Maybe one highly sensitive person always buys the same brands at the grocery store because they are used to that very specific taste and becomes distressed if the store has run out. This preference is somewhat minor but can still cause stress. A more extreme example is refusing to move cities for an exciting job opportunity because they are afraid of transitioning to a new environment. This kind of fear of change has the power to seriously limit your life and hold you back from potentially rewarding opportunities.

It is also important to note that there is a difference between change you have control over and change you don't have control over. Some HSPs may feel that they very rarely have control over any kind of change that occurs in their life. If they can help it, they will not decide to make major changes in their lives because it is too dangerous for their excessive sensibilities. This can be very limiting, but ultimately they are able to mitigate their anxieties this way. However, life also has a tendency to throw changes at us that are outside our control, and for all of us, there is no avoiding this kind of change. This can send an HSP's anxieties reeling. Thus, while you might enjoy a comfortable life living the same routine and not making many changes for yourself, it is important to acknowledge that change comes whether you like it or not and that preparation and confrontation are the only ways of getting through them.

Excessive Self-Criticism

Highly sensitive people are very self-reflective. While this quality has its benefits, which we will talk about in the next section, it can also lead to negative thoughts and self-blaming. The tendency to overthink for HSPs means that they will likely turn these thoughts against themselves and start picking apart everything they do. They might obsess over the way they look or talk, convinced that others notice all of their imperfections and are judging them. Some negative self-talk is normal, but the high sensitivity quality of HSPs means that they will feel these things more deeply and go further with them. In extreme cases, highly sensitive people might avoid social situations because of the extremely negative thoughts they have about themselves, retreating from a world they are convinced hates them.

Food and Medication Sensitivities

HSPs tend to have favorite foods that are very important to them and also have lots of foods they don't like. Because of their heightened taste buds, strong or pungent flavors might actually affect them more strongly than others. Foods like olives, cilantro, kimchi, or other strongly flavored foods might be difficult for HSPs to handle. They might also have a hard time taking certain medications, especially if those medications involve an uncomfortable administration process; swallowing pills, getting injections with needles, or drinking badly flavored cough syrups are some things that highly sensitive people might struggle with. For those with more health problems, these sensitivities to medicine can pose serious threats and might actually require the HSP to find alternative means of taking their medication. For highly sensitive people, food and medicine can be a challenging maze to navigate.

Burnout

The most common difficulty that HSPs face is simply overexerting themselves. You are not lying about feeling overwhelmed; your body is telling you it needs to stop. If highly sensitive people ignore their body's clear signals of overwork or sensory overload, especially on a long-term basis, then they run the risk of experiencing burnout. Make no mistake: Burnout is a serious affliction. It can attack every part of your body from your back to your heart and cause serious damage to your mental health as well. Some people take months or years to recover from serious burnout, and those who leave it untreated can face lifelong consequences. While this all sounds scary, it is merely to emphasize the importance of listening to your body and not pushing your sensitive self past your limits. Everyone's needs are different, and what might be a sustainable workload for one person can be too much for someone else.

THE STRENGTHS OF THE HIGHLY SENSITIVE PERSON

Despite all of the scary-sounding risks above, being highly sensitive is not without its benefits. There are many ways in which highly sensitive people can actually do certain things better than those without high sensitivity. Many HSPs report feeling like their sensitivity actually gives them an advantage in life. While HSPs still have to manage their limitations, they should also be aware of how their sensitivity can be used for good and how they can learn to channel their heightened senses into something helpful and productive.

Here, we will look at how living with high sensitivity might actually be to your benefit.

Intuition

Highly sensitive people are known for having strong intuitive senses. They are able to detect subtleties in emotion, environment, and many other things. HSPs will very often pick up on nuances that most people wouldn't notice or care about. This quality means that HSPs are often overrepresented in fields that require this sort of intuitive thinking, such as psychiatric care and even forensic work. If you're a highly sensitive person, consider using your amazing intuitive abilities to your advantage and applying them to the world.

Soulful and Spiritual Personalities

Back in Chapter 1, we mentioned deep thinking as a sign that you might be a highly sensitive person. This depth of thought can lead to some of the wisest and most soulful people you'll ever meet. Because of the rich internal world of the HSP, their philosophical and spiritual minds run deep and they are able to grapple with the most complex metaphysical questions. You might find that people don't just come to you for advice about emotional problems but for spiritual guidance as well, asking you questions about the deepest aspects of life itself. If you're an HSP, it's highly likely that you have some unique thoughts in this area and can offer a well-considered perspective that others with less rich internal worlds might not have.

Strong Self-Awareness

Even though overthinking can be a burden on the highly sensitive person, it can also lead to a very acute sense of self and awareness of their own personalities. HSPs spend lots of time reflecting on their circumstances and usually come up with very insightful conclusions. If you are one of these people, you probably often get told that you are very self-aware or that you have a strong sense of how your actions affect others. Even though HSPs often fall into patterns of being people pleasers, they rarely hurt others because of their constant self-reflection. For this reason, HSPs can be some of the most caring and considerate people around, hardly ever taking advantage of others or manipulating people. This is one of your greatest strengths and shouldn't be compromised even when you start speaking up for yourself more and setting stronger boundaries. It is important to retain your self-awareness and consideration of others.

Naturally Nurturing

Along the same lines, HSPs often have very strong nurturing instincts. Because they are so good at reading other people, they are also very sensitive to their needs. This quality is especially important when caring for others like children, animals, or the elderly. HSPs make amazing parents and tend to raise children who are also very emotionally intelligent. They also thrive in careers that involve taking care of others like home care workers, pet care, and childcare. Use your caring strengths to your and others' advantage by making sure you have enough people to care for in your life. This will allow the best sides of your high sensitivity to thrive.

Creative

There is a stereotype that poets and artists are all brooding melancholics who can't handle the real world. While this is an outdated and limited idea about creativity, there is some truth to this mythology. Creative people have to delve further than others into the world of emotions and thoughts, look into the deeper aspects of human nature, and consider complex questions. In some cases, this means experiencing emotions in a heightened state to truly cut to the core of what they mean. Sound like anyone you know? Because of their heightened sensitivity, HSPs make great writers, artists, filmmakers, and other creative professionals. Their sensitivity can seem like a curse sometimes, but given the right tools of expression, it can be spun into a blessing not only for the HSP but also for those around them who are privileged enough to gain insight into their minds through their work. If you feel like your emotions are too deep for you to handle, consider taking a page out of Van Gogh's book and channeling those feelings into something beautiful.

3

HSPS UNDER THE MICROSCOPE

S o, you're familiar with all the generalized experiences—the good and the bad—of living with high sensitivity. Now we can take a closer look at the facts and statistics about HSPs and dive into the distinguishing aspects of the condition. In this chapter, we will outline a few specific characteristics of high sensitivity. First, we will look at some interesting facts and research that has been conducted about HSPs, imparting some important knowledge any highly sensitive person should know. Next, we will discuss the intersection between high sensitivity and other conditions that may be similar or have crossover. Finally, we will dispel some myths about high sensitivity that are common in our society. At the end of the chapter, you should be able to connect the more individualized information you learned in the first two chapters to the broader information in this chapter.

FACTS ABOUT HIGHLY SENSITIVE PEOPLE

The study of high sensitivity is a relatively new but well-researched field that has come up with a lot of interesting information about the condition. In this section, we will share some important insights into the research surrounding high sensitivity.

The Term "Highly Sensitive Person" Was Coined in the 1990s by Elaine Aron

Back in the last decade of the 20th century, psychological researcher Elaine Aron identified a common trait between many of her patients: the tendency to respond more sensitively to things than others. In particular, she identified this trait as being independent of other conditions and decided to single it out as its own trait; thus, the term "highly sensitive person" was born. Ever since then, people who experience high sensitivity have the ability to define their feelings.

It Is Sometimes Known as "Sensory Processing Sensitivity"

A more technical term for high sensitivity is the scientifically recognized syndrome of "sensory processing sensitivity." This term has a literal definition and actually describes the central nervous system of the sufferer. According to the research on sensory processing sensitivity, this condition is characterized by people's nervous systems actually working harder than the average person's, meaning sensations and stimuli are felt more intensely, both physically and psychologically (*Sensory Processing Disorder*, n.d.). The physiological properties of sensory processing sensitivity dictate that high sensitivity is actually a physical disorder of the nerves.

It Is Not a Disorder, but a Temperament

Technically, high sensitivity, and even sensory processing sensitivity, are not classified as disorders in the same way that OCD or anxiety are. Neither appear in the Diagnostic and Statistical Manual of Mental Disorders (DSM), and you cannot be formally diagnosed with either. Instead, high sensitivity is a personality feature. You can't be formally diagnosed with it by a doctor, but learning about it can still be an important psychological tool to guide you in your healing process.

Highly Sensitive People Tend to Attract One Another

According to Elaine Aron's research, about half of all HSPs are married to other HSPs. These types of relationships have the potential to be either healthy or unhealthy. On one hand, they can be good because the partners will be able to understand each other more deeply and accommodate each other's needs. However, it can fall apart when both partners' needs become too great. For those HSPs who struggle to do certain basic tasks, it can be a challenge to be with each other, especially when it comes to more practical concerns. Highly sensitive people can flourish together, but sometimes they might be better suited to somebody who can handle more overwhelming situations on the HSP's behalf.

CONDITIONS SIMILAR TO HIGH SENSITIVITY

As we've talked about throughout the book, there are several conditions wherein high sensitivity is either similar to or part of it. These conditions are often confused with or even misdiagnosed as high sensitivity. For this reason, it is important for an HSP to consider the crossover between high sensitivity and other conditions. You might have been misdiagnosed with something else or even have a larger condition of which high sensitivity is a symptom. In the following section, we will discuss the relationship between high sensitivity and a collection of other personality traits and disorders.

Introversion

Though not a disorder by any means, introversion can be closely linked with high sensitivity. Many traits we associate with introversion are also traits of HSPs, such as introspection, social anxiety, rich internal worlds, and more. Perhaps you have been a highly sensitive person all your life but were always told you were just introverted. While you can be both, often people's very real experiences with high sensitivity are downplayed by others as introversion, thus not acknowledging the genuine hardships HSPs face.

Sensory Processing Disorder

Another disorder that relates to the senses is sensory processing disorder, which sees sufferers struggle to take in certain stimuli or information. The key difference is that sensory processing disorder has two extremes: one that is very similar to high sensitivity and one that is completely the opposite. For high sensitivity sensory processing disorder, sufferers struggle to filter sounds or mitigate their reactions to different stimuli, which can look very much like high sensitivity. However, on the other side of the spectrum, some people with a sensory processing disorder will actually struggle to be stimulated at all, being unresponsive to even abrasive stimuli. This presents a whole host of other issues which can actually produce similar outcomes as high sensitivity. If you experience high sensitivity, it's worth looking into whether you might also have an officially diagnosable sensory processing disorder.

Autism Spectrum Disorder (ASD)

Previously divided into autism and Asperger's syndrome, the DSM now categorizes all of these conditions as falling on a spectrum known as the autism spectrum. So, people on the autism spectrum might have extreme symptoms that require intensive care while some have symptoms so mild that they may go unnoticed. Nowadays, with the broadening umbrella of autism spectrum disorder, more people are realizing that the difficulties they have experienced throughout their lives might actually be connected to ASD. In particular, many people who previously thought they were just sensitive or "fussy" are now getting a proper ASD diagnosis, which allows them to identify their symptoms and develop proper coping mechanisms. For many people, this is a lifesaver. They finally feel like they are understood and have a word to describe their complex feelings.

ASD also has some very similar symptoms to high sensitivity; in fact, high sensitivity can actually be one of the primary symptoms of ASD. Often, high sensitivity to things like foods, sounds, textures, and more is one of the first symptoms identified in a person with autism, especially children. High sensitivity is also frequently associated with stereotypical depictions of autistic individuals. It is important to remember that many people just have high sensitivity and are not on the autism spectrum, but if you are a highly sensitive person, you should still reflect on whether you show any other signs of ASD in order to seek the most appropriate and effective strategies to help you manage your symptoms.

Attention Deficit Hyperactivity Disorder (ADHD)

Although it might not seem like it at first, there is actually a strong connection between attention deficit hyperactivity disorder and high sensitivity. We might not associate the introverted, introspective image of the HSP that we've built up so far with the stereotypically chaotic, hyper image of a person with ADHD. However, many people with ADHD actually experience a high degree of sensitivity to their environments. The tendency in ADHD sufferers to alternatively struggle to pay attention and to hyperfocus can actually be related to environmental overstimulation. If you feel like your environment is overstimulating, you might feel an overwhelming urge to flit from one thing to another, your mind overloaded with possibilities. Similarly, you might also want to retreat into a solitary project like painting or writing in order to limit your world and mitigate your overstimulation. When you think about it, ADHD and high sensitivity actually have a very strong relationship. Whether or not you have been diagnosed with ADHD, think about how your high sensitivity symptoms might relate to the symptoms of ADHD.

Borderline Personality Disorder (BPD)

Another mental disorder that has close ties to high sensitivity is borderline personality disorder. BPD is usually characterized by extreme behavior, such as mood swings and manipulation. While HSPs tend not to be manipulative or self-destructive, they often show other signs similar to those with BPD. One important similarity is their emotional instability. Both HSPs and those with BPD tend to have trouble regulating their emotions and can have frequent outbursts or melt-downs. These feelings might be triggered for slightly different reasons, but the outcome might actually look the same.

For this reason, many HSPs are actually misdiagnosed, especially by amateurs, as having BPD. Their loved ones might be frustrated with their behavior and attribute it to a more serious condition than it really is. If you have been diagnosed with BPD but don't feel like you really fit all the criteria—or even still feel misunderstood about your feelings and motivations—consider that you might just be an HSP with your emotional behavior being misdiagnosed and follow up with a professional.

COMMON MYTHS ABOUT HSPS

As with many groups of people who share a unique experience, highly sensitive people are very misunderstood. Not only do they have to deal with constant suspicion from people who think they're faking their sensitivity or that they should just "toughen up," but they also are subjected to some harmful stereotypes. When people first learn about highly sensitive people, they might already start forming some assumptions in their heads. For HSPs, much of their life might be spent dispelling some stereotypes in the minds of others and even themselves. Here, we will look at some of these common myths and explain why they are both harmful and untrue.

Myth #1: HSPs Are Always Introverted

Although highly sensitive people are more likely to be introverted, there are also lots of HSPs who are extroverted. In fact, about 30% of highly sensitive people are actually estimated to be extroverted (*Highly Sensitive Person*, 2022). For this 30%, life can actually be even harder than it is for introverted HSPs. While introverted HSPs can be happy retreating from the world and pursuing more solitary or lower-key lives, extroverted HSPs will likely suffer more due to their difficulties with forming relationships. For the extroverted HSP, the world might be a place that is both alluring and terrifying. They might try to force themselves to engage in things like parties or concerts for the social aspect of it, enduring the pain of being overstimulated. The solution for extroverted HSPs is to find ways to have social interaction without forcing themselves to be in overstimulating environments, such as having more one-on-one interactions or nurturing friendships based around quieter activities. There are lots of extroverted HSPs, and they deserve to be heard!

Myth #2: A Certain Gender Is More Prone to Being Sensitive

There are certain age-old stereotypes about the ways women and men act or should act. Namely, women are expected to be more sensitive than men and be the nurturing members of society. When we were talking about the qualities of HSPs, especially the strengths, back in Chapter 2, many of the things in that section had a direct connection to women's roles in society. Things like emotional labor, being considerate of others, and feeling strong empathy for others' pain are all things traditionally associated with womanhood. Thus, some people may believe that being an HSP is more commonly seen in women, which is not the case. High sensitivity is the same across all genders, although it might manifest differently based on the stereotypes associated with the gender you present as.

These stereotypes hurt everyone in different ways. For women, their sensitivity might be a source of shame at conforming to traditional gender roles. If you are resistant to stereotypical ideas about women, you might find yourself cursing your overemotional qualities and resenting the idea that everyone expects you to be a free therapist or child carer. Embracing your sensitivity can be a complex thing for some women since so many of the HSP's strengths are similar to roles that women have historically been forced into. Perhaps you want to go into a career in a STEM industry but feel that your sensitivity makes you more apt to pursue a career in childcare. All careers are valid, but some women might feel pigeonholed by the particular strengths their sensitivity gives them.

For men, there are many quite different issues surrounding sensitivity. More straightforwardly, plenty of men have been taught their whole lives that sensitivity makes them less important and less likely to earn respect. They were possibly scolded for crying or showing emotion at a young age, leading them to believe that they will be less valued by society if they let their sensitivity show. Many men might also find it intimidating to join careers that are well-suited to HSPs. Male nurses and kindergarten teachers are routinely mocked in the media, making male HSPs feel like they can't play to their own strengths without facing potential ridicule. For some highly sensitive men, pursuing these careers can be quite personally liberating, but they can sometimes come at the price of not always feeling accepted by society.

Suffice it to say, gender and gender stereotypes can play a huge role in an HSP's relationship with their own sensitivity. You might feel differently about being highly sensitive based on what gender you are and might even face more or less scrutiny for your high sensitivity based on your gender. However, it is important to note that HSPs occur at the same rate in all genders and there is no gender prerequisite for sensitivity.

Myth #3: Highly Sensitive People Are Always on the Autism Spectrum

Although we did talk about common symptoms between high sensitivity and autism, there is no actual link between the conditions. That is, while high sensitivity can be a trait of a person with autism, not all highly sensitive people are on the autism spectrum. In fact, if you are just a highly sensitive person and have no other autism symptoms, you are no more at risk than the average person. High sensitivity can often be misdiagnosed as autism, but they are by no means closely related.

Myth #4: HSPs Are Pushovers

Yes, people with high sensitivity do tend to feel more guilt around saying no and will often go the extra mile for other people who may not deserve it. That being said, HSPs are not always pushovers, especially in their own minds. As we've also said, HSPs are actually very intuitive and deep-thinking people. If someone is exploiting them, it is likely they are aware of it. The struggle with HSPs is to articulate these discomforts to others and set boundaries. Even though HSPs might struggle to do this, they are not necessarily pushovers in the conventional sense, merely people who are extra sensitive to others' feelings and let them get in the way of their autonomy.

Myth #5: HSPs Need to Toughen Up

We've talked a lot about this attitude so far, but let's unpack it a little further. We live in a culture that values perseverance and pushing through things even when the going gets tough. These values can be admirable in some cases, but for people who are actually pushing themselves further than they are able to go, this attitude can be toxic. HSPs often fall into this kind of criticism with teachers or bosses or family members in constant exasperation over their perceived limitations. Frustrated people around you might say things like, "Why can't you just stick it out?" or "You're almost done, let's just finish what we started." Hearing this can be so heartbreaking to an HSP, who is feeling these things more acutely than the speaker can imagine.

These kinds of criticisms will often come about when the person attempts to set boundaries and is frequently the reason HSPs have trouble doing so—because people won't let them. Sometimes, these people have a reason to be frustrated. Maybe you and your friend bought tickets to a concert and planned to go together because you wanted to push yourself, but once you get there, you realize that you can't handle it and ask to leave. Your friend might feel rightfully disappointed because they were excited to have fun at the concert with you, but they should also be mature enough to manage their disappointment and respect your boundaries. Remember that your needs and safety come before others' fun even though it can be hard to disappoint them.

Myth #6: HSPs Are Weak

This myth is one of the most misinformed of them all and clearly reveals a lack of knowledge of the HSP experience. If you are truly familiar with how hard it is to live the life of a highly sensitive person, you will know that they are anything but weak. The heightened experiences that HSPs deal with on a daily basis are very real and actually make the HSP much better at enduring feelings of being overwhelmed or overstimulated than the average person. If someone without high sensitivity had to go through a day in the mind of a highly sensitive person, they would realize that it takes a very thick skin to be able to constantly manage emotions of that caliber. Anyone who dismisses HSPs as weak or unable to handle things clearly has no understanding of what they go through.

Myth #7: HSPs Cannot Be Good Leaders

What do we think makes a good leader? Is it someone who is loud? Direct? Aggressive? These might be the qualities of many leaders in our world today, but they do not necessarily reflect the ideal qualities that good leaders should have. If we revise our vision of what a leader should be to someone who can connect deeply and empathetically with the people they are leading, who thinks long and hard about important issues, and who has a strong sense of personal accountability, then we can see how a highly sensitive person might fit very well into that role. The high emotional and intellectual capacity of HSPs means that they are able to very effectively make decisions on behalf of large groups of people. From this standpoint, the world actually needs more highly sensitive leaders, people who are willing to consider the humanity of politics and make every decision intentionally and thoughtfully. So, anyone who says that HSPs can't be good leaders has a very limited view of what a leader should be.

Myth #8: HSPs Are Outwardly Emotional

When we think of someone who is very sensitive, we think of someone who wears their heart on their sleeve, someone who can never hide what they are thinking or feeling. With HSPs, it is quite the contrary. They might have trouble when confronted with an entirely new overwhelming emotion, but they are remarkably good at keeping it together considering the levels of intense emotions they deal with every day. If you really think about it, HSPs are actually experts at controlling their emotions on an everyday basis. They have learned this through years of practice as they needed to develop a variety of emotional coping mechanisms for their day-to-day lives.

People also express emotions very differently. One highly sensitive person might be prone to intense emotional outbursts while another might bottle it up all inside. Many symptoms of things like panic attacks or emotional breakdowns are all internal things only felt by the sufferer. Rushing thoughts, rapid heart rate, chest pains, sweating—none of these things are immediately visible to the outside observer. This can be a good or bad thing. On the good side, many HSPs are able to hide their emotions very well, but on the bad side, they might end up suffering in silence with no one to offer them any help.

Myth #9: HSPs Can't Have Busy Lives

We have been talking at length about the HSP's capacity for stimulation, so it might follow that all HSPs need to have minimally stimulating lives to accommodate their needs. This can be true to a degree; highly sensitive people often avoid environments that can trigger feelings of overstimulation, but this does not mean that they need to lead unfulfilled lives. Given the right accommodations and coping tools, HSPs can live very full lives, taking on lots of projects and filling their time with meaningful activities. Some HSPs prefer a work-from-home lifestyle where they can have more control over their environment and schedule, and some just need to find the right field that suits them and can help them stay busy without risking overstimulation or burnout.

Myth #10: HSPs Can't Be Caregivers

This myth has already been dispelled in Chapter 2, but it's important to restate here. Some people might think that HSPs don't have the emotional regulation skills to handle taking care of others. They think of HSPs as weak people who need to be taken care of themselves, not the other way around. But this simply isn't true. When a highly sensitive person is given the correct situation and opportunity, they can make some of the best caregivers around.

MOVING FORWARD

So, now that you have dug a little deeper into the world of the highly sensitive person, learned some important facts, and dispelled some harmful myths, we can start looking at some coping mechanisms for dealing with high sensitivity. In the next chapter, we will examine some emotional regulation tactics that can help you better live with high sensitivity.

4

EMOTIONAL REGULATION

E motional regulation is one of the most important things for a highly sensitive person to learn. Think of it as a tool in your back pocket to combat your feelings of overstimulation. Most of us learn how to emotionally regulate ourselves as children and young adults. We learn the things that comfort us and begin to recognize the signs that we need to remove ourselves from a situation. Sometimes, we even learn these things subconsciously, intuitively gravitating toward things that will calm us down emotionally. For the average person, emotional regulation is second nature.

But for highly sensitive people, these basic emotional regulation tactics often aren't enough. The general ways most people calm themselves down or channel their emotions are not as effective for highly sensitive people. Furthermore, HSPs often face intense backlash for trying to implement general coping mechanisms since they do it more frequently than others. The average person might have leeway to cancel plans, but for the HSP who might do it frequently, their friends might become annoyed and say things like, "You're always canceling on me." Highly sensitive people need a greater degree of emotional regulation than the average person as well as the tools to communicate these needs to others.

In this chapter, we will share some important tools for emotional regulation specifically geared toward the highly sensitive person. We will explore how you can implement these strategies into your daily life. By the end of the chapter, you should have a better sense of how to manage your feelings of overstimulation and move through life with more ease.

WHY SHOULD YOU PRACTICE EMOTIONAL REGULATION AS AN HSP?

As a highly sensitive person, learning particular emotional regulation techniques is an imperative process without which you will be more at risk of turning to negative coping mechanisms. Peruse this list to discover the key reasons you should work on learning and incorporating strategies to help you miti-gate your heightened emotional states.

Reason #1: As an HSP, You Naturally Feel More Than Others

The first thing to accept when embarking on your emotional regulation journey is that you can't help feeling more deeply and powerfully than other people do. As an HSP, regulating your emotions is not about trying to make them go away or even diminish them; it's about learning to handle them. Let's face it: Your sensitivity isn't going anywhere, nor should you want it to. These feelings are natural and a part of who you are. You can help yourself manage these emotions more effectively without repressing them.

As we have previously talked about, many general emotional regulation strategies simply don't work for HSPs. While the average person might be able to take generalized advice about regulating their emotions, HSPs need to find advice specifically catered to them and their needs. The naturally higher emotional state of the HSP makes it so that they have higher emotional regulation needs.

Reason #2: HSPs Take Longer to Manage Negative Experiences

The experience of the HSP is not just being over-whelmed by crowds but also involves being cut more deeply by certain experiences. Things like breakups, deaths, and even professional setbacks can be more emotionally devastating to an HSP than they would for most people. For this reason, HSPs often react much more strongly than you might expect, often needing to take long periods of time off from work or social inter-actions to rest and recuperate. Besides the initial reac-tion, HSPs often also take longer to recover than people expect. Conventional rules like taking one month to recover from a breakup for every year you were in the relationship don't apply to the HSP. What's worse, these kinds of expectations can end up adding to the HSP's distress by making them feel guilty about their recovery process. Don't let cultural expectations about recovery get you down; recover at your own pace.

Reason #3: HSPs Tend to Fall Into Emotional Ruts

Though it is important to take your time with emotional recovery and recover at your own pace, it is also important to be able to recognize when you are in a rut. Because of the HSP's tendency to overthink and dwell on things, it is easy for them to get stuck rumi-nating about a problem or negative experience for much longer than necessary. If you need some extra time to recover from something, that is perfectly fine. But if you find yourself consumed by something and perseverating on it, that might be a sign that you've fallen into a rut and need to find your way out. Luckily, with some simple emotional regulation tactics, you can work your way through these ruts so negative experiences don't end up controlling your life.

Reason #4: Emotional Regulation Helps You Understand Yourself

If you're a highly sensitive person, you likely already have a strong understanding of yourself. You probably spend a lot of time considering your motivations and dissecting your emotional self. You might even share these thoughts with others or write them down in a diary. However, the specific inner workings of your high sensitivity might still be somewhat of a mystery to you. By learning emotional regulation tactics, you demystify your emotions and allow them to come to the surface. Becoming more aware of these things can strengthen your sense of self and help you help yourself when the need arises.

Reason #5: Emotional Regulation Can Help You Ask For Help

We all have a hard time asking for help sometimes; having the courage to admit we are struggling is something that is difficult for everyone. This is especially true for HSPs who can feel like they are asking for too much help too often. They also might fear being dismissed, misunderstood, or not being taken seriously. Therefore, learning more about your emotions and how to regulate them is crucial to being able to ask for help. If you understand your needs better, you can more effectively communicate what you need and why you need it. The better you know yourself, the better you can help others know you and help you as well.

Reason #6: Emotional Regulation Helps You Be Aware of Triggers

Though you probably already have an idea of what kinds of things trigger your anxiety or feelings of over-stimulation, having a stronger sense of emotional regulation can help you organize those things in a more systematic way. By yourself or with a therapist you can write down all the situations where you have felt overwhelmed and identify some common factors, perhaps even ranking the feelings on a scale of one to ten to determine the severity of the triggers. Having this honest discussion with yourself about what situations are particularly difficult for you can help you be more intentional in the things you avoid, steering clear of scary things and allowing yourself to enjoy the things that don't trigger you.

Reason #7: Emotional Regulation Helps With Decision-Making

Almost everyone has made a major life decision on the spur of the moment at some point. Maybe you spontaneously got married in Vegas or decided to study abroad after a conversation with a friend; maybe you broke up with someone too quickly during a fight or quit your job in a fit of frustration. Whether it was a bad or good decision, many people make decisions based on very temporary emotional states, sometimes ultimately regretting it and sometimes not. For HSPs, their heightened and often turbulent emotions make them more vulnerable to these kinds of spur-of-the-moment decisions. To help improve your rational decision-making, you should make sure you have strong emotional regulation strategies so that you don't make impulsive decisions that you may later wish you hadn't.

Reason #8: Regulating Emotions Can Help Your Relationships

Though HSPs are naturally very good at helping others, sometimes their relationships can become very one-sided in the other person's favor. HSPs run the risk of under-communicating their needs to their friends and loved ones. This can be frustrating for both parties as your friends want to understand you and your needs. By sorting out yourself first, you can then bring your newfound conclusions and personal discoveries to friends to help them understand what makes you tick. Your family, friends, and partners will surely thank you for giving them the proper tools to better understand you and strengthen your relationships.

Reason #9: Emotional Regulation Is Confidence-Building

Most of all, the ability to control your emotions and cope with their consequences will give you a strong sense of autonomy. There's no feeling more powerful than knowing that you can handle anything the world throws at you. Once you've learned to construct coping mechanisms for all the things that might come your way, you will feel an immense sense of confidence in yourself. You can walk out into the world and face it without fear, having the freedom to do as you please and know you can handle it. This is the future all HSPs want—not to get rid of their sensitivity but to be able to manage it well so that they can have the confidence to live full and happy lives.

STEPS TO MANAGING YOUR EMOTIONS

Now that you know why it's important to have healthy coping mechanisms, we can get into what they are. In this list, you will find a wide variety of strategies to manage your emotions and mitigate your feelings of overstimulation. Of course, you will not necessarily need to use all of them, and conversely, not all of them will work for you. Carry this list with you through your daily life and engage in some trial and error. See which things help you and keep those in your back pocket. Learning to manage your high sensitivity is all about finding what kinds of things work for you and going with them.

Step 1: Identify Your Triggers

The first order of business is to identify the things that make you feel overwhelmed and determine what kind of high sensitivity you have. Think back to the last few times you felt overwhelmed. What was the context? Who were you with? What did the environment look, feel, and sound like? Try writing down a full description of these events and look for any patterns. Perhaps you find that family situations overwhelm you, or large crowds, or bright lights. Any pattern that you can discern can start as a guide to mapping out your list of triggers and identifying all the things that make you feel overwhelmed.

Step 2: Evaluate How Those Triggers Make You Feel

After you've described the environments in which you've felt overwhelmed, you should go more in-depth about how you felt during those experiences. This aspect of your journaling will help you consider your particular emotional response tendencies. Do you tend to freeze up? Get irritable? Check out? Cry? Whatever your typical response is to these situations will be the other major factor in deciding what coping mechanisms you should be using. Your emotional reactions to the triggering environments are just as important as what those environments are. Only by investigating both can you start drafting a plan to avoid and conquer overwhelming situations.

Step 3: Remember You Are Regulating, Not Repressing

As we said before, you are not trying to rid yourself of your high sensitivity but rather learn to manage it in certain contexts. Repressing your sensitive emotions is actually a negative coping mechanism and will lead to you having an unhealthy relationship with your emotions. It is likely that you are already repressing your overstimulation and are looking for a way out of it. Just "sucking it up" or "pushing through" will not help you navigate the complexities of what you're feeling, nor will it help you feel better. You need to learn to work with your emotions, not fight them. They are telling you something important, and it is much better to listen than to ignore.

Step 4: Try Different Coping Mechanisms

Once you have primed yourself to better understand your emotions and how to regulate them, you can start trying out some strategies to handle your emotions. Here, we will list some common coping strategies HSPs use for managing their emotions. From this list, think about which ones might work for you and try them out the next time you feel overwhelmed. Remember to record your reactions and how well the strategy worked so you have a better idea for next time. All these coping strategies are things you can do in the moment to try and calm your anxieties and immediately alleviate feelings of overstimulation.

▷ **Breathing Exercises**

One of the most common ways people alleviate anxiety is through breathing exercises. There's a good reason: Breathing exercises target both your mind and body. Mentally, they give you a simple task to focus on by creating a meditative practice of rhythmic breathing that can help your mind reorient itself and escape overthinking. From a physiological standpoint, breathing exercises help physically regulate your heart rate and prevent hyperventilation. By calming your mind and your body, breathing exercises can help bring you back down to earth.

▷ Surveying the Room

Sometimes, being overwhelmed involves feeling disoriented or lost in an environment, especially an unfamiliar one. If you find yourself in that kind of situation, try to take a mental survey of things you can see, smell, hear, and so on. Some people organize the things they are perceiving into numbers using a strategy in which you mentally list five things you can see, four things you can hear, three things you can touch, two things you can smell, and one thing you can taste. This surveying of the senses can help keep them in check, grounding them in your conscious mind and taking some of their power to overload you away. You might find that separating your senses from one another can make you feel more in control of them.

▷ Retreating Into Your Mind

Remember that rich inner world we were talking about before? Now is the time to use it. If you find yourself in a situation that is overwhelming, especially if it doesn't require any physical or mental energy on your part, such as a constraining car ride or a scary movie, consider retreating into your mind. You can think about a story you've been making up, fantasize about an upcoming vacation, or think of any absorbing material that will mentally take you away from your surroundings. This creates a barrier between you and the world and allows you to take charge of your mind's contents. You might find that just a few minutes of this kind of thinking is all you need to recharge your batteries and face the world again.

▷ Removing Yourself From the Situation

This one is definitely not to be used every time. For one thing, you can't always physically leave a situation. There are times when you are (sometimes literally) on an unstoppable train and don't have any means of escape. But when you are in a situation where you have freedom of movement, there is no shame in simply removing yourself. This might be a tough decision, especially at somewhere like a concert where you might not be able to go back, but if you truly feel overwhelmed, sometimes it is best to simply remove yourself. There is no reason to feel weak; you know your limits better than anyone, and if you reach them, leaving might be best.

Step 5: Implement Long-Term Coping Mechanisms

The strategies above are very useful, but they are immediate, Band-Aid-type solutions to your problems. They may help you get through a one-time situation, but they will not fix some of the long-term issues that HSPs face. For example, you might be able to use the room surveying technique to distract yourself from an overwhelming party, but it will not help you communicate with the coworker who has been taking advantage of your accommodating nature. For these deeper problems, long-term strategies are needed in order to build confidence and resistance to sensitivity. Some of these long-term coping strategies will be discussed further in Chapter 8, but they include getting adequate sleep and nutrition, keeping a consistent journal, implementing meditation into your life, and having clear goals. If you combine some of these long-term strategies with the short-term ones, you will be able to address your sensitivity from all angles, building up a strong foundation for your emotional literacy.

Step 6: Learn More About High Sensitivity as a Condition

Congratulations! You're already doing this step. Just by reading this book, you are helping to build up a foundation of knowledge and a tool kit for managing your high sensitivity. It doesn't stop with this book though. There are many other resources for HSPs, including blogs, forums, and online communities that can help you by both allowing you to share your own experiences as well as hearing the experiences of others. Learning about high sensitivity is a lifelong process, and you are only just getting started!

UNHEALTHY COPING MECHANISMS

Unfortunately, as with many of life's challenges, some sufferers turn to unhealthy methods of managing their feelings. These unhealthy methods can range from ineffective to damaging to life-threatening and can actually end up becoming problems in and of themselves. In this section, we will look at some of the common negative coping mechanisms that HSPs use, examining both the reason for their use and the consequences.

Rumination

Thinking too long and hard about topics might not be physically harmful, but it can be very counterproductive to your healing process and, at worst, can lead you into a downward mental health spiral. Rumination is different from merely thinking about something. When you are thinking, talking, or journaling about your problems, you have a purpose behind your actions and hopefully achieve healthy progress in managing your feelings or an event in your life. You might start drawing conclusions, reaching realizations, or inching steadily closer to the truth. With rumination, however, you are not progressing in any linear way. In fact, rumination is an inherently stagnant process. Your thoughts are going in circles, but you don't seem to get anywhere. At best, you will waste your time with rumination, and, at worst, you will create a spiral of thoughts that becomes increasingly irrational and actively prevents you from living your life. Suffice it to say, rumination is not a good way to try to deal with your problems.

Suppression or Avoidance

As we've already discussed, the goal of emotional regulation is not to completely eradicate your emotions but to learn to live with them. Excessive suppression can lead to festering negative emotions and can even start to cause you chronic physical pain. No matter what you do, suppressed emotions will come back in some form, so it is best for them to come up in a controlled environment where you are ready to face them.

Avoidance is another method of suppression that involves simply avoiding any situation where anxieties arise. Now, of course, we did suggest removing yourself from situations where you are overwhelmed, such as a concert. Sometimes, this is necessary for your mental health, and sometimes, it's even necessary to remove yourself from larger situations, such as jobs or relation-ships. Just make sure you're doing these things for the right reasons. Are you removing yourself because you genuinely feel overwhelmed? Or are you avoiding something altogether because you are scared of confrontation or setting boundaries? Make sure that when you avoid things, it's for the right reasons.

Leaning Too Hard on One Person

As an HSP, creating a strong support network is essential. You can't help yourself if you have no one helping you. However, it is important to make sure this support group is wide and varied enough that there is no one person upon whom you depend completely to provide you with support. These expectations are far too much for one person to handle, especially if they are not getting paid. For example, if you frequently need rides to and from the places you go, make sure you have at least three or four people you can call. If you only have one, that makes them feel like a full-time on-call taxi service and might actually make them feel extreme guilt if they are unable to help you at a certain time. So, when choosing people to lean on for support, remember to have a wide net and not just one person to carry that pressure.

Self-Harm and Substance Abuse

On the most extreme end of negative coping mechanisms, some people with high sensitivity turn to drugs or self-harm in order to numb their sensitivity. Substances like alcohol and marijuana in particular dull your senses which can be enticing to someone who feels like their senses are being constantly attacked. For a short time, they can feel more like a normal person and perhaps even enjoy some activities they previously couldn't handle.

However, the consequences of these behaviors soon become apparent. While recreational drugs can be harmless in small doses, using them as a crutch for your sensory issues can quickly lead to a dependence problem. You might soon find that you struggle to spend time with people without the aid of a particular substance. This is very dangerous, even if the substances you are using aren't life-threatening or chemically addictive. Remember that your goal is not to dull your senses but to channel them into something beautiful.

5

SETTING BOUNDARIES

One of the most important—and most challenging—aspects of a highly sensitive person's life is setting boundaries. As we've talked about in previous chapters, it can be difficult to get people to take you seriously and accommodate your needs when you are experiencing sensitivity. With others, you need to learn to make it very clear that your needs are perfectly valid and communicate those needs effectively. In this chapter, we will take an in-depth look at how exactly you can make your needs clear to others so you can build a safe network of people who know how to accommodate your needs. We will also explore ways to build your confidence to say no to people who are trying to push you past your limits.

WHAT ARE BOUNDARIES?

Everyone has boundaries, things with which they are comfortable or uncomfortable. No matter how open you think you are, there are definitely still things you aren't comfortable with people doing to or around you, especially without your consent. Some people don't really like being hugged by strangers, some people are very private about their personal lives, and some don't even like other people entering their homes. Think of boundaries like the fence around your comfort zone separating the things you are and aren't comfortable with. In some cases, you may have people whom you feel comfortable allowing within your comfort zone, but not necessarily. Boundaries can be social, physical, mental, or anything at all. At the end of the day, boundaries are all about making sure you are comfortable with everything you do.

Boundaries are particularly important for HSPs. Typically, HSPs will have stronger, or at least different, boundaries than the average person. There are some common boundaries most people share, such as not taking food off someone else's plate or not going into someone's bedroom unannounced, and they are generally accommodated without question. In contrast, the specific needs of highly sensitive people are often met with skepticism or even ridicule. For example, if a highly sensitive person has strong boundaries around touch and doesn't want to shake someone's hand, they might be viewed as rude or standoffish and perhaps even be outwardly criticized for it. Thus, the different boundaries that HSPs have can make it difficult for them to be accommodated in a world where only more common boundaries are accepted.

TYPES OF BOUNDARIES

Whether or not you are an HSP, you probably have different facets of your boundaries that might look completely different from one another. You might be extremely open and have few or no boundaries in one area of your life, and you might be extremely private in another way. You also might have different contexts in which these facets play out. For example, perhaps you are extremely physically sensitive around strangers but very physically affectionate with your family. In this section, we will connect some of these facets to coordinating boundaries so you can start to explore your relationship with boundaries.

Physical Boundaries

Physical boundaries relate to touch and can apply to any situation from formal work meetings to an intimate relationship. Those who are sensitive to touch often feel that their physical space is being invaded even at the smallest physical contact. You might recoil at the thought of basic social niceties like hugs, handshakes, high fives, or even fist bumps. On the other hand, you may struggle in more intimate settings, which can be even harder. You might dislike hugging family members or holding hands with a partner in public, which can actually lead to seriously hurt feelings. Later on, we will talk a bit more about how to mitigate those feelings.

Physical boundaries can be some of the most powerful and debilitating for an HSP. A sense of bodily autonomy is a necessity for everyone, so making sure your physical boundaries are respected is essential. Most people have their physical boundaries respected automatically, but HSPs have to work hard to set and hold them. Just remember to never let anyone touch you in a way you're not comfortable with and to assert yourself when you feel that your boundaries have been breached.

Sexual Boundaries

Sexual boundaries are somewhat related to physical boundaries, but they are obviously specific to a much more intimate setting. What's hard about sexual boundaries for HSPs is that sexuality is a sensitive topic for everyone, and many people receive inadequate sex education. So, HSPs might have a harder time finding resources for topics around sexual autonomy because of societal taboos. However, it is important, especially for HSPs, to start having these conversations. The more you talk about it, the more the taboo is broken and people can begin to set clear boundaries and be more open about their sexuality.

One other aspect of sexual boundaries for HSPs is that they often feel things more strongly, so sex can actually be a far more intense thing for them. This can be a good thing because HSPs often have very rich and fulfilling sex lives, but it can also mean that certain things that are seen as normal sexual milestones can take HSPs longer to reach. They might take longer to let someone see them with their clothes off or be touched intimately. As with other physical boundaries, it is paramount that you always check in with yourself and make sure that nothing you're doing is making you uncomfortable. If you are with someone who respects your boundaries, you should be able to constantly communicate with them about your comfort level.

Emotional Boundaries

On the other side of intimacy, talking to others about personal things can be as sensitive as physical touch. Emotional boundaries can mean words of affection, expression of feelings, or talking about intimate or personal topics. Again, you might be comfortable with these things in some contexts but uncomfortable with them in others. There might be certain settings, such as your own home, where emotional intimacy is easier for you, or maybe you feel more comfortable on a trip when you are separated from familiarity. You will also likely have certain people with whom you feel more comfortable sharing your emotional self, possibly due simply to their receptiveness to you or perhaps because of your closeness or history with them. It's important to know that you don't owe anyone emotional intimacy, and if someone is pressuring you to tell them things you don't want to, that is just as invasive as touching you without your consent.

There are a few sides to emotional boundaries. First of all, you should be able to express only the feelings you want to express. You might be comfortable talking about your issues with your family but want to keep issues pertaining to your love life more private. This might come as a shock to some people who might see you as a very open person because you've talked about one facet of your emotional life in the past only for you to freeze up when a different topic arises. Be conscious of what issues are more sensitive to you, and make sure you don't share anything you aren't comfortable sharing.

Another side to emotional boundaries is being able to express them without ridicule. For HSPs, this is particularly important since they are more vulnerable to criticism than others. Being open emotionally is one of the most vulnerable things you can do and can have extreme impacts. On one hand, being received well can be incredibly fulfilling and validating; someone finally recognizes you and understands how you feel. On the other hand, being received badly can cut deep, especially for an HSP, and possibly lead to a future aversion toward emotional intimacy. For this reason, it is imperative as an HSP to choose your confidantes wisely and make sure your vulnerabilities will be received well and treated with respect.

Religious or Spiritual Boundaries

Religious beliefs are intensely personal. Furthermore, they often intersect with daily activities, either minutely or significantly. Whether you're very devoted to your faith and follow all the fundamental rules of your religion or you're a deeply spiritual person who doesn't necessarily adhere to organized religion, faith is an important part of who you are. Boundaries also tend to come into play in particular with religions that have specific prayer times or dietary restrictions. In a more secular society, or if you are a religious minority, you might have faced ridicule, disrespect, or even persecution for your religion. Thus, setting boundaries around your religious and spiritual practices is very important in order to feel comfortable and protect yourself.

As we discussed in Chapter 1, highly sensitive people tend to be very deep thinkers and are often deeply spiritual. They often have strong commitments to their faith and feel these things profoundly. For this reason, it is very important for HSPs to establish strong boundaries around their religious practices. It might be something as small as pointing out that you can't go to a steak restaurant with your friends because you don't eat beef or making sure you have time to pray at the appropriate times at work. Even though you might face some backlash from people in your life, the depth of your commitment to your spirituality means that you should never compromise it. As an HSP especially, your time for reflection is more important than anything, so you should be intentional about making that a priority in your life.

Time Boundaries

On a related note, many HSPs feel that having time alone to recuperate after an overstimulating situation is very important to them. Thus, you will likely need to set clear time boundaries with people in your life. This might mean that you have to forgo certain commitments or cut certain events short. You might not be able to go on a weekend getaway with friends because it won't allow you enough downtime. It's important to recognize that needing this downtime doesn't mean you're antisocial; it just means that you have different social needs.

Another facet to time boundaries is using your time wisely. As we stated in Chapters 1 and 2, HSPs often have trouble saying no to people or refusing work. You might find yourself taking on projects in your workplace that others wouldn't, often for no pay increase. Even if you are very passionate about your work, everyone has a limit, and if you are overworking yourself, you have found your limit. The inability to refuse extra commitments is a sign of poor boundary setting. It's fine if you want to work hard but be sure that you never feel pressured into taking on anything that you're not comfortable with.

Financial Boundaries

One of the more awkward aspects of adult life is that everyone inevitably has different income levels and expenses. Furthermore, even if you know how much money someone makes, you never know how much of that money they're able to spend. You might have a friend who makes twice as much as you but has a house, a car, and three kids, and therefore they may have less spending money than you. If you find yourself in a group of friends who have more disposable income than you, it can sometimes be very awkward to make plans. They might want to take a week-long group trip to the Caribbean that isn't in your budget. For HSPs, it can be especially hard to say no to making plans like this, and they may even find themselves living beyond their means to try and keep up with friends. Even though it might make you seem like a killjoy, you should always try to make your budget clear and not succumb to peer pressure.

WHY ARE BOUNDARIES IMPORTANT?

Comfort might seem like a luxury, but it is actually a basic human right. What you are and are not comfortable with has a considerable influence on your life. Of course, breaking out of your comfort zone as an experiment can be a rewarding experience, but constantly engaging in things outside of your comfort zone can be harmful. When you're trying to expand your horizons, what you're really doing is trying to expand your comfort zone. If you know something is uncomfortable for you and you do it anyway, you are neglecting yourself. Here, we will look at some of the reasons why setting boundaries is a very important part of any highly sensitive person's life.

Reason #1: Protection

When it comes to more serious issues like privacy and autonomy, boundaries are incredibly important. Whether it's establishing when you are comfortable being touched or how much information you are willing to share with someone, boundaries can actually protect you from potentially dangerous or traumatizing situations. While it is never the victim's fault when they encounter a boundary-pushing situation, you can boost your personal safety by being aware of your boundaries and communicating them as best you can.

Reason #2: To Take Back Control Over Your Life

Likely, if you're a highly sensitive person who struggles with boundaries, you sometimes feel like your life is outside of your control. People are always pushing you to do things you don't want to do and taking up your time. If this is your situation, setting boundaries can be a very liberating experience as you are finally asserting control over your schedule and your life. For those who are former people pleasers now living more autonomous lives, boundaries were their way out.

Reason #3: To Avoid Burnout

We talked a lot in Chapter 2 about how HSPs are prone to burnout because of their people-pleasing tendencies. Setting boundaries can help you manage your time as well as your mental and physical health much more effectively. If you sense yourself starting to burn out, you can turn your boundaries up a notch and avoid falling into that vicious cycle of overexertion and crashing. In order to avoid burnout, boundaries are your first line of defense.

Reason #4: To Boost Self-Esteem and Learn About Yourself

It's likely that if you are the people-pleasing kind of HSP, you probably don't give your own needs enough care and consideration. Establishing boundaries can not only be freeing but actually self-defining. Many people find the work of figuring out their boundaries to be an act of self-discovery as they are finally asking themselves difficult questions they have never really thought about before. You might find yourself saying, "You know what? It does make me uncomfortable when my mother makes those comments," or "I actually don't really like the volunteer work I'm doing, and I just keep doing it because I feel too guilty to quit." Realizations like these can only come up when you engage in self-reflection, and for a lot of people, this happens the first time they truly try to set boundaries.

HOW TO SET BOUNDARIES AS AN HSP

Now that we've established why boundaries are important and what they can do for you, we can start to look at the steps required in creating boundaries. You will probably find boundary-setting to be both a very liberating and very arduous process. It might help you learn some fundamental things about yourself, but it also might compromise your relationships and force you to do some deep and difficult inner work. Through this process, you will discover what is truly important to you and who you truly are. If you find these steps too difficult, make sure to take breaks and step away from the process. You don't want your journey to fight overstimulation to be overstimulating in itself!

Step 1: Look Inside Yourself

The first step to setting boundaries is to figure out what those boundaries should be. As with figuring out your sensitivities, journaling is a great place to start. Think about some times when you felt uncomfortable or overwhelmed. Write down what happened and how it made you feel. Then, write a new version where you think you might have been more comfortable. What changed? Were you in a different place? With a different person? In a different state of mind? Once you ask yourself these questions and compare and contrast your real and imagined experiences, you can start drawing lines in the sand as to where your boundaries might be. Similar to discovering your key triggers, discovering boundaries requires extensive introspection and reflection on past experiences.

Step 2: Set Boundaries Only With Yourself

Before you start creating boundaries for other people, consider starting with some that only involve yourself. For example, maybe you always go into work 30 minutes early but you have identified that as something that causes you stress. Since this decision only affects you, you might start coming only 15 minutes early or on time. People might notice, but you are not asking anything of them. As another example, maybe you find crowded bars overwhelming but find yourself at one every weekend; you can make a promise to yourself to find somewhere with a different type of atmosphere to socialize, such as a coffee shop or a bookstore. These kinds of boundaries will start to build a base for the limitations you will put into place going forward and will put you on a path toward better self-care.

Step 3: Take a Small Step With Interpersonal Boundaries

No matter how many individual boundaries you set, at some point you will eventually have to establish some boundaries with other people. The best way to do this is to start small with people you're not as close to. For instance, say you always pay for gas when you carpool with your coworker. They've never offered to pay, and you've always stayed silent. Perhaps one day you can politely ask them if they could contribute and gauge their reaction. These small acts of boundary-setting in lower-stakes relationships and situations can be a good place to start building confidence before tackling the bigger issues in your life.

Step 4: Move Onto the Most Important Boundaries

After setting and maintaining some smaller boundaries, you will have gained a sense of autonomy and confidence in your abilities. You may have encountered some difficulties, but hopefully, the low-stakes nature of your early boundary-setting experiences has allowed you to try new things in a riskier setting; now it's time to try applying those things in a more intense context. Consider the first experience you wrote down in your journal during Step 1. Why do you think you wrote it down first? Unless you have dealt with it already in Step 2 or 3, the first thing you wrote down is likely the most important thing to you or the thing that impacts your life the most, so you should start with this one as the first major boundary you set. Maybe that means telling a friend it makes you uncomfortable when they are too touchy-feely or telling your boss that you actually can't take on that extra project. These things might seem scary, but you can think back to the boundary work you have already done and how confident and empowered it made you feel. If setting those less consequential boundaries made you feel relieved, imagine how you will feel when you set some even more important boundaries!

TIPS FOR SETTING BOUNDARIES

These steps might sound scary at first. Telling people the things you've been afraid to tell them for years? Breaking commitments that you have felt so obligated to keep? Standing up to your intimidating boss? You might be saying, "I'm a highly sensitive person, remember? Those things scare me more than anything!" You're completely right: Even starting small and building to more important boundaries can still pose risks. Here, we will look at some extra tips to ease your anxiety about boundary-setting and help these transitions go more smoothly.

Tip #1: Remind People It's Not Personal

One of the hardest parts about setting boundaries, and likely one of the main reasons that setting boundaries is scary to you, is the worry that you might offend people. Telling someone you can't help them out or that you can't spend as much time with them as you have in the past can elicit some extreme reactions. People might feel like you don't like them or that you're rejecting them. These dynamics can get especially messy with more intimate relationships. So, while your friend might be more understanding about you not liking hugs, your spouse might not feel the same way. The more intimate the relationship, the more likely you are to offend with boundary-setting. But—and this is critical—these intimate relationships are the most important places to set boundaries.

So, how do you set boundaries and minimize hurting others' feelings? The most important thing is to remind the person you're with that your boundaries have nothing to do with them and don't reflect the nature of your relationship. Perhaps you can educate them a bit on high sensitivity using some material from earlier in this book, mixing it with personal stories about your own triggers and experiences. Reaffirm the relationship you have and let them know that they are not to blame and that you don't care about them any less. If you make this clear, you can alleviate hurt feelings and help the people in your life understand where you're coming from. If the person rejects your boundaries, even with careful reassurance and explanations, then they likely weren't a good fit for you to begin with. If you are successful, you will actually strengthen your relationship as they will understand more about you and what you are comfortable with.

Tip #2: Take Their Boundaries Into Consideration

As we said at the beginning of this chapter, everyone has boundaries. Your friends and partner presumably have their own sets of boundaries that they may or may not have shared with you. Their boundaries might also play a role in the boundaries you set. For example, maybe you feel like you can't drive your spouse to work anymore because it is too far out of the way, but they struggle with crowds and don't like taking public transportation during rush hour. When these conflicts arise, try to remember that both of you are attempting to establish boundaries and communicate your needs. Work together to reach a compromise that will meet both of your needs instead of merely stating your boundaries and expecting them to blindly accommodate.

Tip #3: Be Consistent

Once you set a boundary with someone, the best way to make sure they respect it is to consistently reaffirm this boundary. Of course, we can't always know how sure we are about something before we have tried it. You might find that you actually miss the talks you were having with your spouse in the car on the way to work or that you don't know what to do with your time now that your work schedule has eased up. These are very real possibilities, but once you have settled on the boundary that you would like to set, it is best to be consistent. For example, if you decide that you don't like bars and don't want to go to one ever again but your friends keep inviting you to pub nights, make sure you consistently refuse. If you say no one night but succumb to pressure and say yes on another night, they might think you actually like these nights more than you really do. Being firm and consistent is the best way to communicate the seriousness of your boundaries with others.

Tip #4: Start Boundaries as Early as Possible

The earlier you start enforcing a boundary, the likelier it is to be respected. While this tip does not apply as much to existing relationships that may already have patterns that violate your boundaries, it is still important to consider at what point in a relationship you should start enforcing a boundary. So, whether you are meeting a new person or starting a new job during this process or not, it is always best to start enforcing boundaries as soon as possible. The longer you continue to tolerate boundary-crossing behavior with the people in your life, the more they will think it is okay and the more difficult it will be to ever enforce a boundary. Make sure you establish boundaries right off the bat with new people and as soon as possible with people already in your life.

Tip #5: Keep Your Boundaries Simple

Like we said in Tip #3, the more consistently you apply the boundary, the more likely it is to be followed. This rule goes for simplicity as well. The simpler your boundary, the likelier people in your life are to follow it. Take the previous pub night example. Say you want to compromise with friends so you agree to join one pub night a month. While this might seem like an appealing compromise, it is actually complicating the boundary and still making you do something you don't want to do. Your friends might forget how often you're doing the nights and continue to invite you weekly or not take your aversion to this activity seriously. A better strategy for compromises is to completely change the nature of the activity. So, continuing with the pub example, you might say, "I really enjoy spending time with you guys, but I just don't feel comfortable in this environment. Can we do some cafe afternoons instead? Or weekly movie nights?" By moving the activity from its original location and changing it to a completely different activity, you are creating a simple solution to the problem. You aren't confusing people with "sometimes" or "if I feel like it," making them feel like they have only one foot in the door. Instead, they understand you are saying, "I don't like this activity, but I value our relationships. Let's exchange it for another activity." Simple, effective, and easier to manage.

Tip #6: Make Your Boundaries Realistic

If you're anything like the typical people-pleasing HSP, you probably don't need to hear this one, but it's still worth stating. Sometimes, even if your boundaries are completely valid, they won't be realistic for every situation you are in. For example, say you have taken on a huge project at work but are feeling very burnt out. You want to stop doing it, but there's no one else who can take it on and the clients are expecting a delivery. Even though it might be the healthiest choice for you to back out, there is no realistic way for you to do so. If this is the case, try your best to finish out any outstanding necessary work and make a commitment to yourself not to take on any more projects like that in the future. In a perfect world, we would all be able to prioritize our mental health every day, but sometimes that's just not an option, and we need to be able to adapt and persevere.

Tip #7: Write Down What You Feel

Not everyone can be brave on the spot. Sometimes we pluck up the courage to confront someone, but once we arrive, we find ourselves tongue-tied. This is especially common with highly sensitive people who might feel overwhelmed once they are in the context of confrontation. They might suddenly become aware of the other person's feelings and then recoil in guilt. A good strategy for this is to write down all the things you want to say to this person. If you have known this person to be argumentative in the past, consider writing down all the arguments you anticipate them making and coming up with rebuttals for each. If you are particularly concerned about how this interaction will go, you can also consider doing it over the phone with your notes in front of you. This way, you can quite literally read from the script and stay focused on your goal. You will also be less susceptible to excess sympathy or guilt that prevents you from expressing your concerns and needs. Be very deliberate about what you are saying and make sure you are able to say everything you feel.

6

SCENARIOS AND SCRIPTS

Love yourself enough to set boundaries. Your time and energy are precious and you get to decide how you use them. You teach people how to treat you by deciding what you will and won't accept.

— ANNA TAYLOR

Now that you've learned all about how boundaries work and why they are important, we can start exploring some of the ways in which you can tactfully set boundaries. As we stated at the end of the last chapter, writing down the boundaries you are attempting to set with the people in your life is an effective way of getting started, keeping yourself on track, and holding your ground. In this chapter, we will take a look at some of the more specific ways to set boundaries with people, giving you some more specific scenarios and scripts you can implement in your own life.

SCENARIOS

There are many different aspects of your life in which boundaries might come into play, and no two boundary-setting conversations will look the same. However, you can learn from similar situations and translate them to your own situations. In this section, we will offer some specific scenarios in which boundaries might need to be set and how to go about setting them in that context.

Scenario #1: Asking for Alone Time

Whether it's with a partner, friend, or family member, every relationship needs its space. Problems can arise, however, when the people in the relationship have different ideas about what that space should look like. Maybe you are very introverted and have a very extroverted friend who always wants to hang out. Maybe your parents still think of you as their precious child and expect you to visit them every weekend even though you live and work full time in another city. Expectations about how much time you and another person should spend together can often be mismatched. For HSPs in relationships, this often means that the other person gets to decide the parameters because of the HSP's sensitivity to others. This can create very one-sided relationships, so the ability to establish strong boundaries is essential.

One strategy for setting these boundaries is to put the emphasis on your alone time rather than on your lack of time with them. Emphasize the importance you place on your time to recharge and feed your soul instead of saying that you want time away from them. If you make it clear that you need more time to take care of yourself, this will take some of the personal hurt away. Try saying something like this to your extroverted friend: "Hey, I love hanging out together, but I have also fallen behind on my reading list. Reading is really important to me, so I think I need to dedicate more time in my week to that which might mean I have a little less time to hang out." For your mom who wants you to visit every weekend, you might say, "Mom, I have such a good time when we're together, but last weekend I had some errands to run that I ended up not having time for. I'm concerned I'm not dedicating enough time to my own household and have been neglecting cleaning and laundry. I think visiting every other weekend might be a better schedule for me so I can keep my own life in check." Both of these scripts highlight the neglected aspects of your life and frame the distance as something you don't necessarily want but do in fact need. If you let someone know that there is something else urgently demanding your attention, they will be less hurt that you are spending less time with them.

Scenario #2: Checking Inappropriate Behavior

Another difficult thing many HSPs have to deal with is calling people out when they cross certain boundaries. Say, for example, you have a friend who always kisses you on the cheek when you meet up. Maybe you feel this kind of thing should be reserved for family members or partners and it makes you uncomfortable when they do it. Or perhaps your boss often addresses you with terms of endearment like "sweetheart" or "darling," which makes you feel uncomfortable. Both of these situations might be instances where the other person may not know they are making you uncomfortable, thus it might hurt their feelings if you tell them their actions makes you uncomfortable. Remind yourself that your comfort is the most important thing and that they probably still want to know the truth.

When trying to communicate about these issues, refrain from using strong words like "creepy," "invasive," or "uncomfortable." These words might make the other person feel embarrassed or bad about themselves, so you should instead try to emphasize your personal feelings and comfort level. This personalizes the boundary to you and doesn't place judgment on the person's behavior in itself. So, for the friend example, you might say something like, "For me, kissing on the cheek holds a slightly more intimate connotation. It's okay if it's something friendly for you, but for me, it is more for family." For the boss situation, you might say, "Those words are a little familiar for the level of professionalism I like to keep." Both of these statements don't insinuate that you think the person needs to stop this behavior altogether, only that they need to stop doing it with you. It can minimize making them feel judged by focusing on how you feel rather than what they do, but it also makes it clear that it's something you're not personally okay with.

Even if you feel that the behavior is objectively wrong, you are likely not in a position to change that person's behavior with everyone in their life, especially if they are an authority figure as in the boss example. It is up to the other people in their life to set their own boundaries. Maybe if enough people set the same boundary with them, they will change their behavior permanently, but you have no control over that, and it is not worth wasting your time trying to change someone. All you can do is make known the things that aren't okay with you and hope they respect your boundaries.

Scenario #3: Declining Work

Whether in a volunteer or professional setting, HSPs are at a higher risk for overwork and burnout. Many HSPs really struggle to set professional boundaries. As a result, they often end up setting a precedent that they are willing to work more than others and end up getting assigned more projects. This can create a vicious cycle of extra work that can lead you straight down the path to burnout. Your coworkers might not be aware that you can't handle this workload and may even assume you enjoy it. In fact, communicating that you need to tone it down might actually shock or annoy them.

When tactfully declining work, make sure to let people know that they haven't been burdening you, nor do you resent the work. Luckily, with this kind of boundary, you don't run too much of a risk of emotional damage. Unless you work for a very small company and have a very close relationship with your boss, there aren't likely to be any hurt feelings. Still, you should remain tactful. Try saying something like, "I am starting to feel my work-life balance slipping. To maintain a better balance, I need to take on less work going forward." Avoid shaming the company or insinuating that they are overworking you. All you need to do, as with setting other boundaries, is make it clear that these boundaries are for you personally and don't necessarily apply to the rest of the employees.

Scenario #4: Drinking Limits

Food and drink, especially alcoholic drinks, can be a very personal thing for everyone. Furthermore, if you're someone who has ever dealt with an eating disorder or a substance abuse problem, this personal relationship can be even more complicated. Imposing limits on eating or drinking can be one of the hardest things to do. Binge drinking is often normalized in American culture, and the choice not to drink or to drink moderately can actually cause you to face some social backlash. Navigating your way through a pub night with people who chronically pressure you to drink can be a minefield of feelings. For an HSP who might be affected more strongly by alcohol, this can be an extremely difficult context in which to set boundaries.

The first rule is to never shame the other person for their own choices. As we have acknowledged, consuming alcohol can be a very personal choice and no one likes to be told they drink too much. So, make sure that when you're setting your boundaries around alcohol, you emphasize that these choices are very personal to you. Try saying something like, "I know that I have a low tolerance, and if I keep going, I might feel sick. Just looking out for my own personal health," or "Alcohol is something I have some anxieties around, and I think if I go any further it might trigger those anxieties." These two phrases limit the boundary around alcohol to you alone while still keeping it firm.

Scenario #5: Parenting Boundaries

Another one of the most sensitive things in a person's life is their parenting choices. This kind of challenge can be particularly exacerbated when friends, family members, or even strangers pass judgment or try to interfere with your parenting style. Perhaps your own parents tend to take liberties with your kids by doing things like giving them candy that you wouldn't let them eat or showing them movies you deem inappropriate. While these things can sometimes be a harmless treat, repeated exposure to these kinds of behaviors can actually work to undermine your authority as a parent. You might also encounter this kind of treatment from strangers who might criticize how you are disciplining your child in public, giving you looks or making comments like, "Your child is spoiled," or "You shouldn't always give him what he wants." These comments also undermine your authority as a parent and can really hurt, especially for an HSP. Setting boundaries is very important for this facet of your life.

Again, reinforcing your own autonomy is key here. You aren't judging their parenting style or even contradicting their opinion. You are just setting boundaries for criticism. Some things you can say to your parents might be: "I know these are the kinds of things you think are okay, but I don't approve of them for my child. I feel like my child might not respect my rules if he sees another parental figure doing something different," or "I think we can consider ourselves a team with parenting my child and should present a united front since conflicting rules can be difficult for a child to deal with. How can we come up with some compromises so that our rules are more consistent?" These two statements acknowledge the discrepancy without judging the other person and move toward a solution that benefits all.

WHAT TO DO WHEN OTHERS DON'T RESPECT YOUR BOUNDARIES

Let's face it, no matter how good of a boundary-setter you become, there will always be people unwilling to respect them. You might face some ridicule for your boundaries or have people who continue to cross them even if they have been asked not to. This is completely normal and doesn't necessarily mean you're a bad communicator. Some people take longer to accept boundaries, and some are inconsiderate and maybe not worth keeping in your life. Here, we'll go over a few ways you can maintain or reinforce your boundaries when others are disrespecting them.

Reminders

Everyone needs reminders every once in a while. Depending on how established your pre-boundary patterns were in a particular relationship or situation, you might have an adjustment period. Someone you used to go out with every week might take a few weeks for the reality to sink in that you won't be doing that anymore. Your mother might still call you to pick her up "just one last time" even though you already said you would no longer be able to do so. Your boss might slip up and say, "Thanks, darling," when you are leaving a meeting. If any of these happen, it's imperative that you don't let them go. Even if it is an honest mistake, you need to nip it in the bud. Similar to how you need to set boundaries as early as possible, you also need to consistently maintain the boundaries and be 100% firm about them right away. If any of these situations occur where someone tries to undermine your boundaries, politely remind them of the boundary you have set previously. The best way to do this is to reiterate a shortened version of what you said originally or refer back to it in some way. So, you could say, "Remember last week when I said that I wasn't able to do this anymore?" or "The issues I brought up last week still stand." This reaffirms your boundaries without making the person feel bad.

Set Even Stronger Boundaries

Sometimes, when you set a boundary that people aren't respecting, it's because you haven't gone far enough. As we stated in Chapter 5, setting boundaries that are simple and clear-cut will have the best results. Essentially, it's best not to go halfway on a boundary but rather to set it firmly and completely. If you find that people are exploiting loopholes in your boundaries or pressuring you to loosen them, then you might have unintentionally set a weak or unclear boundary. While it can be tempting to loosen the boundary to appease people, it's actually better to set an even stronger boundary. So, for example, if you had said you wanted to hang out "less often" with one of your friends, that is fairly open to interpretation. An open-ended boundary like that leaves room for your friend to push back on your boundaries until things are eventually back where they started. At this point, you might have to introduce some concrete rules. Consider saying something like, "When I said less often, I meant more like two or three times a month. I'm sorry if we weren't on the same page about that." The way this is phrased suggests that the boundary-crossing was the result of a mere miscommunication, allowing you to reclaim control over the situation and call back to your original boundary while pushing it further and making it more concrete.

Besides solidifying your boundary with more concrete or specific language, it might also be necessary to take the boundary to the next level. This can apply to the pub night example. If you originally stated that you only wanted to go out once a month instead of once a week, your friends might exploit this allowance and start asking you more often. If this happens, you might have to escalate the boundary and change the location of the hangout to somewhere you feel more comfortable such as a cafe. Escalating the boundary is a good response to the person exploiting a weakness in your boundary. Of course, your boundaries should always be determined by your comfort, but you might actually have to limit yourself more than you would have in order to cover all possible loopholes. Even if you would be okay with being at a pub once a month, it's not worth it for the pressure you might receive.

Gauge Their Willingness to Change

One of the most important parts of dealing with people who are having trouble respecting your boundaries is determining their reasoning for doing so. A lack of respect for boundaries can come from a lot of different places. When you find someone pressuring you to break your rules or engaging in behavior you asked them to stop, ask yourself what their intentions are. Do they not care? Are they forgetful? Are they having trouble understanding your boundaries? Do they not fully understand your reasoning for setting these boundaries? Do they feel offended by your boundary-setting and want to punish you by disregarding them? Reflecting on the motivations of these people is integral to resolving these conflicts over boundaries and determining how forgivable their boundary-crossing is.

Some examples of forgivable boundary-crossing might be forgetfulness, lack of understanding, or lack of ability. For genuine forgetfulness, they will likely just need some thorough reminders and the boundary should eventually sink in. Lack of understanding might be a little more difficult, but in the best of cases, some clear and direct communication can clear up most misunderstandings. Open up a discussion with them where they're free to ask you questions (within your comfort zone, of course) and answer them to the best of your ability. Hopefully, in the end, they will have come to a better understanding of how your boundaries work and will respect them more going forward. Finally, the lack of ability will be the hardest aspect to manage.

Sometimes, the person actually needs something from you and doesn't know where else to get it. Other times, people have a genuine social inability. For example, you might say to your mom, "It hurts me when you only talk about yourself and never give me a chance to speak." It might not actually be within her ability to let you talk about yourself due to her own personal or mental health issues. In these cases, you have to take a serious look at whether your boundary is something they are even able to respect and whether that is something you can deal with.

Some less forgivable examples of boundary-crossing are not taking you seriously, taking the boundary personally, trying to override the boundary with your relationship's closeness, or making it about themselves. Not being taken seriously is one of the hardest things HSPs have to deal with, and it is especially prevalent when trying to set boundaries. People not taking you seriously is very hurtful, and you should make it clear to the person that your personal sanity and relationship with them are on the line if they don't start respecting your boundaries. The person might also wage emotional warfare with you; this is particularly common with parents who might see your boundary as an attack and use guilt against you. Again, if this continues past the point of reasonable communication, you have to remain firm and state that your relationship is on the line. All of these reasons are not well-intentioned, but hopefully, with some strong messaging, you can find a way to make them understand your point of view.

Consider Cutting Them Out of Your Life

No one wants to go no contact with anyone in their life. Losing a friend or family member is an extremely painful experience that can leave lasting damage on all parties involved. Obviously, this is a last-resort solution and should only be done if you have tried every possible way to get them to see the value in your boundaries. If you have discussed, communicated, reminded them, and even upped the rigidity of your boundaries to no avail, then you need to take a serious look at their role in your life. Weigh out the level of discomfort their boundary-crossing causes you against the value of their relationship. Having a mom who calls you too much might be something you can learn to live with, whereas a boss who verbally abuses you at work should not be. At the end of the day, you have to decide how much discomfort you are willing to tolerate for the sake of your relationship with that person.

One tool for this is to write a journal entry about what your life would look like without them. Take a context in which they are usually there (for example, one of your friends in a group, your sister at a family dinner, etc.) and write a version of that context where they aren't there. Reflect on how their absence makes you feel. Do you feel relieved? Sadness? Peace? Grief? Doing this imaginative work can help you see the value in their role in your life as well as in your comfort and autonomy. If your imagined life without them is more peaceful to the point where it overrides your missing them, then you might have to consider cutting them out of your life. This is a painful process that will require a whole other book to help you through it, but for some people, it is the only option to mitigate their over-whelming sensitivity in certain situations or with certain people and keep their autonomy.

MAKE PEACE WITH THE THINGS YOU CAN'T CHANGE

We've mentioned in this section thus far the unfortu-nate reality that not everyone will be willing or able to meet your needs, yet you will still have to keep that person in your life. Sometimes, the people who can't or won't respect your boundaries are too valuable to you to sever contact with completely. Hopefully, you are strong enough to only keep around those who truly mean a lot to you and not just those for whom you feel bad, and that the boundaries they are crossing don't threaten your physical safety, bodily autonomy, or mental health. Sometimes, little boundary violations from extremely important people in your life who won't back down just have to be tolerated. It's an unfortunate reality, but it happens. Here is some advice on how to make peace with these things.

Set the Boundary Within Yourself

Even if you have not been able to make someone see things from your point of view, you have still done so much inner work to control your emotional state. You have likely discovered more about yourself and identified the things that make you feel uncomfortable. You might have also undone years of self-deception around your own feelings and are for the first time acknowledging your truth about things. Despite external circumstances, you have still set an emotional boundary and are no longer lying to yourself and others that you are okay with things that you actually aren't. Hopefully, with this mentality, you will be less affected by boundary-crossing in the future and can take more active measures to regulate your emotional reaction.

Never Tolerate the Behavior or Back Down About How It Makes You Feel

Letting someone stay in your life doesn't have to mean pretending everything is okay between the two of you. In fact, it is very important to be firm in your boundaries and never back down for the rest of your relationship. You don't owe them the sacrifice of your boundaries just because they won't respect them. Make sure that every time they violate your boundaries, they know they have done so, and don't try to reassure them about it. You won't help your relationship by quietly tolerating their disregard for your comfort. Perhaps, over time, they will finally be able to respect your boundaries. But even if they never do, you should still stand your ground and never deny your own feelings or lie to make them feel better.

Reinforce the Boundary Periodically

In addition to never backing down, you should also try to have periodic conversations in which you remind them of your boundary. This should look like the initial conversation you had but with added examples from the interim. While you should try to point out every boundary violation as it happens, this isn't always realistic. If you can't do this, bring up examples of times they violated this boundary during your check-in and try to illustrate as best you can how it made you feel. Again, this consistency might slowly change their mind, but even if it doesn't, it should give you clarity and catharsis to be honest about how you feel with them.

Try "Little Contact" Instead of "No Contact"

You don't have to cut someone out of your life completely to reduce their impact on you. While little contact does leave room for those pressures we talked about with loose boundaries, it also offers an opportunity to maintain a more distanced relationship with someone who hurts you. Consider moving to a different city so that you only visit on occasion or changing workplaces so that you only have to see them if you meet up. Distancing yourself from a person can offer some of the benefits of no contact without the hard cutoff. In some cases, this can be the ideal setup and might actually improve the relationship.

7

HSP SUPERPOWERS

In Chapter 2, we talked about some of the strengths highly sensitive people possess including strong intuition, creative minds, and deep empathy. Even though there are a lot of ways in which HSPs are challenged in the world, there are also these very important things that come more naturally to them than the average person. As an HSP, you have the power to change the world using your unique set of skills. In this chapter, we will examine how these superpowers can be used.

CREATIVITY

As we've talked about throughout the book, HSPs are known for being very creative. They think very deeply about topics and can come up with some of the most unique ideas. Due to their philosophical and even spiritual nature, HSPs make amazing artists, writers, and other creatives; some of the most famous creatives of all time have been HSPs, a testament to the potential people with this personality type have. If you're an HSP, you should seriously consider letting your creative side shine. If you're already expressing yourself creatively in some way, try to channel more of your unique sensitivity into it, and if you're not, consider taking up a paintbrush and trying it out for yourself!

Introspection

One of the reasons HSPs are so naturally creative is because of their intensely introspective minds. One might say that the best artists are merely those who think longer and harder about subjects than the average person, coming up with a more interesting and nuanced perspective. For HSPs, thinking is their middle name. HSPs can overthink to a fault, but it can really do them well when working on creative projects. They will likely come up with truly reflective ideas that can become brilliant poems or stories, even creating visual art that has a distinctly deliberate quality to it. From their ability to think very pensively about pertinent philosophical concepts, HSPs draw a beautiful creative voice.

Personal Fulfillment

Some HSPs actually find their creativity to not just be a perk to their sensitivity but also an important way of dealing with it. Their creativity causes them to muse deeply about important topics as well as about themselves. The trademark self-awareness of HSPs often originates from creative work. Channeling their sensitivity into a creative project can be a great outlet in addition to an opportunity for self-discovery. If you are an HSP, you can use your creative abilities to fulfill yourself personally and discover new things about yourself that you never imagined.

At Work

You don't just have to be creative in your spare time. Work offers lots of opportunities for creativity. Even if you don't work in a creative field, you can always inject a bit of your creative mind into your professional life. Whether you're a curator at an art gallery or head of mergers and acquisitions, that HSP touch is always appreciated. You likely have some of the best ideas to share, shining on projects where you have to design something or communicate with others. If you make the most out of this professional creativity, you will dazzle your bosses and become one of the most valuable members of your team.

INNOVATION

Related to creativity, innovation is another great strength of the HSP which can be put to fabulous use. The unique thought process of the HSP means that they are able to come up with things that no one else would have dreamed of. For this reason, HSPs make great inventors and problem solvers, excelling in fields like software design. When it comes to new ideas, HSPs are constantly pushing the envelope.

Thinking Outside the Box

Due to their innovative natures, HSPs tend to think far outside the norm on many topics. You might find yourself pitching ideas that your coworkers wouldn't have ordinarily suggested. You'll probably look at problems in a slightly different way, seeing a deeper connection and using your natural intuition to access something beyond what's expected. If you're working on a team project, you can be an amazing asset with your lateral thinking and deep introspection.

Using Your Unique Perspective

As an HSP, you actually have a unique experience in the world. You can offer a distinctively creative perspective that might be overlooked in ordinary practice. Beyond offering these innovations, you also offer the HSP perspective and can use your voice to speak up for the HSP community. This is especially useful if you are inventing marketing products where you can consider the HSP customer and their reaction to certain products. Bearing in mind that you can't speak for every HSP, you can still offer an important perspective when in a room of non-HSPs.

HELPING OTHERS

HSPs are known for being people pleasers, which can be hard on them, but if controlled properly, it can also be their superpower! With firm boundaries in place, HSPs can use their strong empathy skills to care for others in their personal lives and even in their careers. HSPs are some of the best listeners and emotional problem solvers in the world, and their skills are much appreciated by friends, family, and even patients who benefit from their strengths. Here, we will look at how HSPs can use their brilliant interpersonal skills to benefit others.

Intuition

As we mentioned in Chapter 1, HSPs often report knowing things will happen before they do or knowing how someone is feeling before they are told. This intuitive quality means that HSPs can often help people with things they didn't even know they needed help with. Sometimes, when you go to someone for advice, you might be a little nervous to bring up some of your issues. HSPs are astute at sensing things like this, making them some of the best people to go to for advice or emotional help.

Standing Up for Others

HSPs often put others before themselves because their intense empathy causes them to feel others' emotions as if they were their own. This quality can sometimes cause HSPs to neglect themselves and struggle with boundaries, but with the right emotional tools, it can be channeled into something amazing. HSPs are often fierce defenders of their friends and never let someone's idea go unnoticed or their feelings go unacknowledged. HSPs will often stand up for other people before they stand up for themselves, making them team players in all facets of life.

8

HSP TIPS

Life as a highly sensitive person can be overwhelming, but the good news is that there are lots of things you can do as an HSP to improve your quality of life. The first thing you should always do is educate yourself about high sensitivity. This book is a great place to start, but there are lots of other resources you can refer to. In this chapter, we will look at some short-term and long-term tips for improving your quality of life as an HSP.

QUICK TIPS

If you're just coming to terms with your sensitivity, then you'll likely not have existing systems in place that help you in your life. You might be immediately struggling and desperately looking for a way out. Of course, long-term solutions should be implemented as well, but you'll need some short-term ones to tide you over for now. In this section, you'll find some solutions that will help you with high sensitivity that can be implemented right away.

Prioritize Rest

Relaxation and recuperation are some of the most important tools in your HSP toolbox. You can't go out and face an overstimulating world or recover from an emotionally exhausting day without being well-rested. Right away, you should prioritize getting at least eight hours of sleep a night as well as making room for timed intervals for rest throughout the day. These intervals will be determined mainly by your type of sensitivity. If you're sensitive to overwork, make sure you take breaks at your job if you can. If you're sensitive in family environments, then designate some time for yourself to be alone and rest after seeing family. Whatever your sensitivity, make sure that you have both an adequate night's sleep going in and time to recuperate afterward.

Have Space for Yourself

One aspect of prioritizing rest is having a place to rest. For ideal rest conditions, HSPs need a quiet, safe place where they can be alone. That can be a bedroom, an apartment, or even an office space if it has a closing door. This situation might not be possible for everyone as not everyone lives alone or has their own room. If you share all your spaces, see if you can arrange a time where no one else will be home or at least not enter that space so you can rest alone. Creating a space for you to be by yourself is integral to creating an ideal HSP rest environment.

Limit Caffeine

Caffeine is a great way to start the day and is one of the most popular and widely used drugs in the world. However, it is known to increase anxiety, making it a potential hazard for HSPs. If you can help it, try to drink as little caffeine as possible. Doing so can exacerbate existing anxiety issues and make your sensitivity worse. Instead, try to find more nutritious ways to give yourself energy including eating healthy snacks like fruit and nuts. You might find that starting the day with an apple and a pack of cashews is actually better for your energy than a coffee!

Limit Light

Light is one of the most common sensitivities for HSPs. Obviously, you can't control public or outdoor spaces, but you can control your presence in them as well as the light in your own spaces. For your home or room, invest in some quality blackout blinds for the mornings or naps and soft lighting for relaxing before bed. You'll probably find that having an incandescent lamp beside your bed will gear you up for sleep much better than a fluorescent overhead. In public or outdoor spaces, wear sunglasses and stay in the shade. Try also to limit time spent in brightly lit spaces or anywhere with strobe or flashing lights. Limiting your exposure to certain kinds of light will reduce overstimulation and help keep you relaxed and calm.

Wear Noise-Canceling Headphones When You Can

Noise is another big sensitivity. While, again, you can somewhat control the noise in your own space, you cannot in public spaces. If you take public transportation or work in a loud office, purchase some high-quality noise-canceling headphones so you can create a sense of auditory tranquility even in an overstimulating environment.

Give Yourself Permission to Be Emotional

If you've accepted that you're a highly sensitive person, you are also accepting that you are emotional. Repressing how you feel will not make your sensitivity go away. Thus, you need to start giving yourself space to be emotional. This might mean letting yourself have a long cry when you need to, venting to a friend after a hard day, or expressing yourself through creative means. Being an HSP means being emotional, and there is no shame in letting these feelings out.

LONG-TERM TIPS

After implementing your short-term tips, you should begin investing time and energy in your long-term solutions to high sensitivity. Here, we will look at some solutions which involve life-changing actions that will take longer to cultivate. Taking these suggestions to heart probably means making major changes in your life, but that's all part of supporting your sensitivity.

Build a Strong Support Network

You can't always do it alone. Depending on your needs as an HSP, admitting your boundaries and sensitivities might mean limiting yourself. You might have to decide not to do things that you need to do and will need someone to support you to help get them accomplished. Support networks are also necessary for emotional support. Deciding to embrace your emotions and be more vulnerable means you're going to need more people to listen to you and give emotional support. Reach out to people in your life while also creating new networks. These people can be friends, family, partners, therapists, teachers, or anyone who is close to you whom you trust and is willing to do the work to support you and take you seriously.

Don't Compare Your Life to Others' Lives

This is good advice for anyone but is especially important for HSPs. Accepting limitations may mean missing out on some things. Maybe you decide to stop flying, attending concerts, or hosting get-togethers in your home. Whatever boundaries you set or limitations you impose on yourself, you will likely be missing out on something, and this can cause mixed feelings. On one hand, you're glad you don't have to do these things anymore—they were likely not enjoyable for you and caused you a lot of stress. However, sometimes you just can't shake the feeling that you're missing out. Friends might post pictures of events on social media, you might lose touch with some casual acquaintances, or you might not be getting in on a project at work that all your coworkers are collaborating on. It can be bittersweet since these things might still have brought you some joy despite being overstimulating. It's important to know that you did the right thing and to try not to feel like your life is any less enjoyable than others' because you don't do certain things.

Take a Slower Pace in Life

As an HSP, the best pace for your life is a slow one. You have probably been living at too fast a pace so far, and slowing down is the best thing to do for your mental health. Even if your problem is overstimulation, not pace, slowing down has a myriad of benefits for HSPs. For one, slowing down gives you more time to recharge between activities. As we talked about before, rest is essential for HSPs, and slowing down your pace of life is one very effective way to make room for rest in your life.

9

THE SUPPORT SYSTEM

Your beauty is in your sensitivity. Don't let anyone take it from you.

— YASMIN MOGAHED

F lipping the perspective, let's take a look at HSPs from an outsider's perspective. Whether you're an HSP yourself or have one in your life, this chapter will help illustrate how to build strong relationships with highly sensitive people while respecting their boundaries and supporting them through their difficulties. You will learn how to talk HSPs through their problems, stand up for them in difficult places, and pay attention to their verbal and non-verbal signs of discomfort. With all the above in mind, let's take a look at how others can support the HSPs in their lives.

GENERAL METHODS OF SUPPORT

There are many very simple ways anyone can support an HSP in their life. Whether that means literally helping them with something or merely changing your behavior to accommodate their needs. Just the fact that you are reading this means you care about a highly sensitive person in your life, so you should make sure to follow these steps to show that care through your actions.

Educate Yourself

It's good to hear advice that you're already doing. Learning about high sensitivity from books, blogs, and other sources is an essential step in understanding the HSP in your life. Try reading personal accounts written by highly sensitive people to get a sense of how the HSP in your life might be feeling. Do some research into mental health resources in your area to learn further about how your HSP can be supported by others as well as you. Basically, you want to get your hands on all the information you can find in order to be as well-informed about high sensitivity as possible. Education is the best way to broaden your perspective and bridge the gap between you and the HSP you care about.

Learn Their Triggers and Remember Them

Of course, education does not end with a general overview. You also need to learn about the specific needs of the HSP in your life. Ask them to share with you all the situations in which they feel overstimulated, making sure not to violate their privacy while doing so. If they are a private person, limit this discussion to any possible overstimulating environments that you might have experienced together. Keep track of these contexts and try to remember them as best you can. This is important for two reasons: The first is that it can help you avoid putting your HSP in a situation they aren't comfortable with. For instance, if they say they don't really like skin-to-skin contact, you can make sure you avoid touching their skin going forward. The second reason is that you can help protect them should they come into a situation that triggers them. Using the above example, you might notice someone trying to shake hands with your HSP and can then politely let them know about their discomfort. This creates a united front and allows the HSP to feel supported in not having to always set their boundaries for themselves. If you are aware of all your HSP's potentially triggering situations, you can be sure to never intentionally put them in one and help them when one arises.

Learn Their Coping Mechanisms

Your HSP knows best when it comes to dealing with their own triggers. In addition to learning about the situations in which they become overstimulated, ask them about the ways they deal with these feelings. Their coping mechanisms might not be what you expect, so don't try to impose your own ideas or suggest things that work for you, especially if you are not a highly sensitive person. If your HSP has done the internal work laid out in this book, they should know when and how they need to be helped in a situation. Your job is to support or facilitate their specific coping mechanism by offering a safe place, a person to talk to, a ride home, or anything they might need. If you're consistent about this noninvasive help, your HSP will learn that you are a person they can trust.

Don't Take Anything Personally or Make It About Yourself

It can sometimes be shocking to have someone set a boundary with you. It might make you question your previous behavior in the relationship and make you feel guilty for crossing a boundary in the past. This isn't necessary. You weren't aware of their feelings before and had no way of knowing how your behavior was impacting them. The important thing is that you always respect their boundaries and never question them once you learn them. It's also important to always keep the conversation focused on them, centering on their feelings and not your own. If you make the conversation too much about yourself, you risk making the HSP feel guilty for setting boundaries. In all likelihood, your HSP already feels guilt and sensitivity regarding your feelings. It is your job, then, to make sure not to take anything they say to heart and know that they wouldn't bring these things up if they weren't deeply affecting them.

Let Them Lead the Way

As we have discussed, your HSP knows what is best for them. They are the best judge of when they need help or need to remove themselves from a situation. Make sure you are aware of this when you are spending time with them, especially if you are their ride or might have had to cut your evening short if they become overwhelmed. Be prepared to drive them home at any time without complaint and try to hide your disappointment if possible. HSPs are very aware of the effect they have on you and may even already be feeling guilty. Try to help them manage their feelings by letting them lead the way. Also, make sure you have enough time apart from them so that you can do the things you want to do without someone needing your support in order to keep your own mental health in check. Say you like going to live music shows but your HSP friend often has to leave early; try to attend some live shows without them on occasion so you can still have a good time without worrying about taking them home early.

However, a situation might also arise where your HSP suddenly wants to do something that they've previously stated is outside their comfort zone. In this case, you should still let them lead the way. Don't try to remind them about a boundary they've previously set if you notice them breaking it. You should also try not to be angry or frustrated that they are "changing their mind." If they decide to make an exception, accept that decision. As long as you don't notice them being pressured, they should be able to take the lead even if they are acting outside the norm.

Stand Up for Them

Not everyone is as committed to supporting HSPs as you are. In all likelihood, you will encounter a situation where your HSP is being pushed beyond their comfort level and is visibly overwhelmed. Because of their high sensitivity, they might have a hard time expressing this themselves. If you aren't an HSP yourself or you have different sensitivities, you should be their cheerleader in this situation. Use your position to stand up for your HSP and let others know when they are crossing boundaries. Your HSP will be grateful to not have to be the one always setting and reinforcing boundaries for themselves. Presenting a united front can also make the person bothering your HSP feel less powerful. If your HSP has someone on their side reinforcing their boundaries, they are less likely to be bullied into violating their own comfort zones.

Respect Their Space

Often, when an HSP starts setting boundaries with you, it means spending less time with them—not always, but this is a very common boundary. Depending on how important they are in your life, this can feel like a real loss. However, as we said above, you should try your best not to take this personally. They are setting boundaries because they need to recharge, not because they don't like you or because you did anything wrong. If those boundaries do include less frequent visits, think about how this affects your life. Are they someone you spend a lot of time with? Do they play a significant role in your life? Will you miss out on some important social time because of this boundary? If any of these things are the case, you will need to find another way to fill the role this HSP has been filling in your social life. This is very important as it will prevent you from trying to pressure your HSP into breaking their rules and also help keep them from feeling guilty. Whatever activity you usually do together, try to find someone else to do it with. If you used to go to concerts together, find someone else who likes concerts and invite them to one. If you used to go on road trips, try finding a new road trip buddy to go on a trip with. Filling your life with more people will help assuage the loss of time with your HSP and strengthen your relationship. Remember: You are not losing them or becoming less close, only changing the nature of your relationship to better accommodate your HSP's needs.

Always Be Transparent and Try Not to Change Plans

Many HSPs experience anxiety when plans are changed or when they aren't aware of all aspects of a situation. Often, to judge whether they will be comfortable at an event, they will need a lot of information about that event, such as how many people are attending, how loud it will be, how long it will take, and so on. Failing to notify your HSP about an aspect of an event you are attending, especially if you know it is related to one of their triggers, can put them at serious risk. When dealing with someone who can be set off very easily, it is imperative that you give them as much forewarning as possible.

Offer to Help With Tasks They Find Overwhelming

Sometimes, HSPs have certain necessary chores that they struggle to do. They might not like going to the grocery store, driving at night, making appointments over the phone, or any number of things. Though they are probably managing these things themselves by creating their own coping mechanisms that allow them to live independent lives while avoiding triggers, everyone can use help. Let your HSP know that you're someone they can call if they need a hand. Give them a specific list of things you're able or willing to help them with along with your availability. And, as always with an HSP, remind them that this is something you really want to do and are not being put out by helping them. They may be afraid they are bothering you, so remind them firmly that they aren't. Lending a hand to your HSP with overwhelming tasks is one of the pillars of your role as a part of their support system.

Check In Often

Your HSP will not always let you know when they are overwhelmed. Sometimes, you have to directly ask them. There are two sides to this: The first side is checking in periodically when you are at an event together that might be potentially overstimulating by periodically asking if they are feeling overstimulated and if there's anything you can do for them at the moment. This opens up a conversation and allows them to express how they might be feeling without bringing it up first. The second side is persistent and regular check-ins. Every once in a while, as frequently as you see fit, open up a deeper conversation with your HSP about how they are doing in general. This can include questions about their workload, social obligations, and boundaries. You should also include yourself in the conversation and ask for your HSP's honest opinion about your level of support. Take any constructive criticism seriously and try to implement any needed adjustments going forward. Again, this allows your HSP to share their feelings without initiating the conversation and to voice their concerns without fear of judgment.

HSP DON'TS

By now, you should be well-informed about the things you can do for your HSP, but what about the things you should try to avoid doing? Just as important as learning how to support your HSP is learning what behaviors can be harmful or invalidating. Here, we will look at some behaviors that might put your HSP in danger or put your relationship with them in jeopardy.

Don't Take Advantage of Their Kindness or Listening Skills

HSPs are naturally great listeners, which makes them amazing friends, but they don't always have the time or energy for others. If you have an HSP friend with whom you frequently have meaningful conversations, consider how much emotional energy they are giving you and how much you are giving them. Commonly, HSPs feel that their relationships, especially those with non-HSPs, tend to be one-sided when it comes to emotional support. Thus, even the most considerate of their friends can get swept up in their amazing advice. Ask yourself if you hold the same amount of space for your HSP as they hold for you. How often do you ask them how they are feeling? How much do they talk about their feelings in comparison to how much you do? Asking yourself these questions will help you gauge whether you are taking advantage of your HSP emotionally. The good news is that if this happens to be the case, you don't necessarily have to have fewer emotional talks with your HSP, just make sure that you are giving them the same attention they are giving you.

Don't Rush Them

HSPs are often perfectionists, worrying over every single aspect of the things they do from projects they work on to events they host. If you are working with an

HSP or are near an HSP while they are working, one of the worst things you can do is rush them. If you are responsible for them or are their supervisor, try to find ways to extend the project or offer solutions rather than rush your HSP through their tasks. From a social perspective, you should also be patient with your HSP. Maybe it takes them a little bit of time to prepare before entering a party or a dinner. Perhaps they take extra time to park their car perfectly. Whatever their preference, it's important to remain patient and try not to make them feel rushed. Like always, let them take the reins.

Don't Surprise Them

Surprises, especially gifts, are generally great. There are many ways you can surprise your HSP like with a thoughtful gift or by spontaneously covering the dinner bill. However, surprising them with an event or a trip can actually end up having the opposite effect of what you intended. Depending on how much notice they have or how far outside their comfort zone it is, these kinds of surprises can actually end up causing your HSP a lot of stress. If you want to do something like this with your HSP, consult with them beforehand, and if you want to surprise them, consider a gift that does not come with obligations.

Don't Hold Them to Non-HSP Standards

We all judge each other by our own standards. We think, "Is that something I would do?" or "How might I react in this situation?" But with an HSP, especially if you aren't one yourself, you can never truly know what is going on inside their head. They often struggle with things that come easily to most people, thus you can never judge the way they react to situations based on the standards of non-HSPs. They have their own emotional standard that non-HSPs may not be able to understand.

RAISING A HIGHLY SENSITIVE CHILD

A guide to parenting highly sensitive children could be an entire book unto itself. Children with high sensitivity have completely different needs than other children. Furthermore, many of the signs listed at the beginning of the book manifest slightly differently in children. All children are more sensitive to things like loud noises and crowded spaces, so it can be hard to recognize whether or not your child is more sensitive than is typical. You might try to compare them (non-competitively) to other children their age. Notice if your child is doing things differently, reacting more strongly, or choosing not to participate in activities other children are enjoying. If these things are the case, you might have a highly sensitive child. Here, we will look at some brief tips on how to support your highly sensitive child and help them grow up knowing how to support themselves.

Accept Their Sensitivity

Your child's sensitivity isn't going anywhere. This might be a hard thing to accept, but think back to all the positives we have shared about high sensitivity and recognize that it can actually be a superpower. This acceptance must be extended on both a small and a large scale. You should accept them as a sensitive person on the whole as well as by showing patience and understanding for their small instances of sensitivity throughout each day. Learn that there is no point in telling them to "toughen up" or "stop being sensitive." This will only force them to repress their sensitivity and no longer think of you as someone with whom they can be honest. Dismissing their feelings will only damage your relationship, which isn't good for either of you. Yes, the world is a tough place, but the best way to prepare your child for it is to give them proper tools to manage their sensitivity themselves, not to try and make it go away.

Try to See Things From Their Perspective

As the adult in the situation, you have emotional tools and resources your child doesn't, even if you don't realize it. You have the ability to self-soothe, talk yourself down from anxiety, and communicate with others —things you have slowly and subconsciously learned throughout your life. You also have more freedom than your child to be able to remove yourself from situations, decide what and when to eat, and refuse to attend events. Because of your increased autonomy, you are actually much better equipped to manage your sensitivities than your child. Because of this, it's important to realize that they are not always being unreasonable. You wouldn't enjoy going hungry, attending a party with people you don't like, or staying somewhere long after you're tired. Understand that your child has neither the emotional tools nor the autonomy of an adult and therefore cannot help themselves as you can. With this in mind, you can better sympathize with your child when they seem unreasonable.

Cultivate Their Emotional Intelligence

Because you have these added adult tools, you can make an intentional effort to impart them to your child. Reflect on your own coping mechanisms. How do you react when you are uncomfortable in a situation? What kinds of things do you do to help yourself calm down when you are feeling stressed? If you have healthy coping mechanisms yourself, you can try to teach them to your sensitive child from an early age so they will have this added guidance when they need to help themselves. As we stated in the last section, it is also important to let the highly sensitive person—or in this case, child—lead the way. If you tend to confront people who are bothering you but your child prefers to remove themself from a stressful interaction, then let them do that. You can try to show them some of your coping mechanisms, but they will naturally gravitate toward their own, and as long as they aren't unhealthy or harmful, they will be what works best for them.

Accept Their Implicit Boundaries

Children don't really have the language or emotional maturity to set boundaries in the way adults do, especially with their parents. Furthermore, part of parenting is helping your children break out of their comfort zone and disciplining them when they refuse to do important things, so trying to respect the boundaries of your highly sensitive child can be tricky. A general rule of thumb is to try to encourage your child to do things they haven't done before but allow them to refuse if it's something they've tried and decided they didn't like. You should also always respect their boundaries when it comes to bodily autonomy, even if it's something they haven't tried before like hugging a family member they're meeting for the first time. By following these rules, you should be able to foster a good sense of autonomy and boundaries in your child while helping them learn and grow as an individual.

The other issue with boundaries and children is that, while they do sometimes vocalize their needs and wants, other times they don't. This could be because they don't know how or because they are scared. However, this does not mean that they don't try to communicate their boundaries subconsciously. The main way that children communicate boundaries is through body language and visible fatigue. If someone tries to hug your child and they physically recoil then comply, this might be an indication that they didn't really want to hug that person but felt like they had no choice. Try to learn the ways in which your child communicates boundaries and notice them when they occur. This will help you recognize when your child is in need of support.

Make Sure They Have Structure and Downtime

For the highly sensitive child, life can feel like a whirl-wind. They are constantly being surrounded by things that are not only bigger and louder than them but that are also new to them. Thus, for highly sensitive chil-dren, overstimulation might lurk around every corner.

They will often try to combat this uncertainty by establishing order within themselves and constantly questioning you about plans or circumstances. The best way to support them in this is to give concrete answers to these questions and even to be proactive about informing your highly sensitive child of plans. Adding structure and a daily routine to their life with clearly outlined activities and times can also help your child emotionally prepare themselves for everything life has in store for them. Make sure you also include lots of downtime in this routine so that they have time to recuperate as well as to prepare. Creating consistency and structure in your child's life is an important aspect of supporting their sensitivity and allowing them to better regulate their emotions.

CONCLUSION

If you're a typical highly sensitive person then it's likely this book was somewhat overwhelming for you to read at times. You might have recognized emotions or tendencies you've never noticed in yourself before. You may also have read through scenarios that you have experienced and might have even found triggering. Hopefully, you have taken some of the book's advice while reading it, pacing yourself and taking breaks as needed. Ironically, coming to terms with your high sensitivity can actually be a very sensitive issue. Don't worry if you've had to pause reading this book or do some emotional work while processing these issues. Your high sensitivity is important to learn about, but you shouldn't push yourself too far too fast.

So, what have we learned about high sensitivity? One of the most important takeaways from this book is that high sensitivity is not a bad thing. You may have been dealing with unrecognized or unaccommodated high sensitivity for a long time which may make it feel like a bad thing. But if you have the proper systems in place, you can turn your high sensitivity into a great thing. In Chapter 2 and Chapter 7, we looked at ways in which your high sensitivity actually gives you an advantage in the world, both personally and professionally. We live in a world that is not kind to sensitive people and often values things like toughness and even cruelty. While you can't change the world, you can find ways to not only survive as a sensitive person in this insensitive world but to thrive. So, while managing some of your more difficult symptoms, also make use of your sensitivity and try to play into its advantages as best you can.

Two key understandings you need to take away from this book are the importance of boundaries and the importance of rest. These two things encompass the bulk of living and accommodating yourself as an HSP. We have talked at length about how to incorporate these two things into your life, but it's important to again highlight that they are arguably the two most impactful ways to manage life as an HSP. Most of the accommodations for HSPs fall into one of these two categories, boundaries encompassing preventative measures and rest providing a means for recuperation. There are some other aspects, such as emotional care and coping in the moment, but boundaries and rest form the foundation. They will be the most important things to emphasize, and establishing them is the most important step in your HSP skill-building.

Boundaries are all about setting limits on yourself and with others. These are all measures designed to prevent you from getting into a situation that might trigger your high sensitivity. Boundaries can be anything from telling friends you can't hang out to telling yourself you can't take on another work project. Boundaries can even involve setting schedules for yourself and planning out your days and weeks to avoid overstimulation. Essentially, a boundary is any step you take to limit, prevent, or plan out your life in order to better manage your sensitivity. The main skills required to impose successful boundaries are effective communication with others and self-regulation. Self-regulation is needed to stick to the schedules you are imposing, making sure you stay consistent and firm in your plans. Communication with others and self-regulation are needed in order to make sure your needs are accommodated while also standing your ground. By establishing emotional, time, spatial, and environmental boundaries with yourself and others, guided by strong communication and self-regulation,

you can create a strong cushion against overstimulation.

The second aspect—rest—is integral as well. Your
boundaries, whatever they may be, will try as best they
can to prevent you from experiencing overstimulation,
but it is inevitable. Life happens and things don't always
go according to plan. People might not acknowledge
your boundaries or you might be forced into something
you don't want to do. As much as you make the effort
to reduce this possibility, it will still sometimes be
unavoidable. Even daily routine activities or activities
you have planned in advance might prove to be overstimulating or at least warrant some kind of rest afterward. Rest addresses the other side of overstimulation,
which is recovery. You should have clear plans about
what you need after an overstimulating situation and
how to implement that need. Maybe you need to lie
down after work every day or listen to some quiet
music after spending time with friends. You should
have a clear plan of action so that when you are overstimulated, you are ready to give yourself what you
need to recover. Through this clear, two-pronged
approach to high sensitivity, you will have all bases
covered in handling and preventing overstimulation.

If you enjoyed this book, or it helped you in any way,
we would really appreciate you leaving us a review.

Share your honest opinion about how this book's descriptions measured up to your experiences with high sensitivity so that other potential readers might find something of themselves here. Try out some of the coping mechanisms we have shared and report back on how they helped you. Interacting with us helps continue the dialogue around highly sensitive people, building up the already-strong community of people who experience high sensitivity. You are now a part of this community—welcome to the world where we see high sensitivity as a superpower. Now get out there and use it!

REFERENCES

Aletheia. (2018, September 17). *The sensitive person's guide to emotional regulation (in 10 minutes or less)*. LonerWolf. https://lonerwolf.com/emotional-regulation/

Anderson, C. H. (2021, May 27). *13 easy phrases that will help you set healthy boundaries*. The Healthy. https://www.thehealthy.com/mental-health/healthy-boundaries/

Andrade, S. (n.d.). *Council post: the importance of setting healthy boundaries*. Forbes. https://www.forbes.com/sites/forbescoachescouncil/2021/07/01/the-importance-of-setting-healthy-boundaries/?sh=606d6d4f56e4

Are you sensitive? Here's why it's a superpower and how to work it. (n.d.). Ellevate. https://www.ellevatenetwork.com/articles/10166-are-you-sensitive-here-s-why-it-s-a-superpower-and-how-to-work-it

Aron, E. (2019, January 22). *Graceful boundaries—Part I*. The Highly Sensitive Person. https://hsperson.com/graceful-boundaries-part-i/

Being "highly sensitive" is a real trait. Here's what it feels like. (2018, August 28). Healthline. https://www.healthline.com/health/mental-health/what-its-like-highly-sensitive-person-hsp

Being sensitive is a superpower—Here are 5 ways to use it. (2017, June 13). Psych Central. https://psychcentral.com/blog/being-sensitive-is-a-superpower-heres-5-ways-to-use-it#1

Boyer, A. (2021, April 29). *8 things you should never do to a highly sensitive person*. Highly Sensitive Refuge. https://highlysensitiverefuge.com/8-things-you-should-never-do-to-a-highly-sensitive-person/

Brunet, B. (2022, June 1). *How to live your best life as a highly sensitive person*. Highly Sensitive Refuge. https://highlysensitiverefuge.com/how-to-live-your-best-life-as-a-highly-sensitive-person/

Bjelland, J. (n.d.). *Common HSP positives & challenges*. Julie Bjelland.

https://www.juliebjelland.com/hsp-blog/common-hsp-positives-amp-challenges

Connell, L. (2021, August 27). *Avoid doing these 9 things to a highly sensitive person.* Highly Sensitive Refuge. https://highlysensitiverefuge.com/avoid-doing-these-9-things-to-a-highly-sensitive-person/

Daniels, E. (2022, January 19). *5 things to know about dating a highly sensitive person.* Dr. Elayne Daniels. https://www.drelaynedaniels.com/5-things-to-know-about-dating-a-highly-sensitive-person/

Daniels, E. (2022, January 19). *10 almost unbelievable benefits of being a highly sensitive person.* Dr. Elayne Daniels. https://www.drelaynedaniels.com/10-almost-unbelievable-benefits-of-being-a-highly-sensitive-person/

Davis, T. (n.d.). *Emotion regulation: definition + 21 strategies to manage emotions.* The Berkeley Well-Being Institute. https://www.berkeleywellbeing.com/emotion-regulation.html

Difference between a highly sensitive person and borderline personality disorder. (2017, October 6). Psych Central. https://psychcentral.com/pro/exhausted-woman/2017/10/difference-between-a-highly-sensitive-person-and-borderline-personality-disorder#1

8 reasons being highly sensitive is actually a good thing. (2018, September 5). Highly Sensitive Refuge. https://highlysensitiverefuge.com/being-highly-sensitive-good-thing/

8 things to know about dating a highly sensitive person. (2021, April 7). Healthline. https://www.healthline.com/health/relationships/dating-a-highly-sensitive-person-hsp#hsp-defined

The 11 most common myths about highly sensitive people. (2020, August 25). Tiny Buddha. https://tinybuddha.com/blog/the-11-most-common-myths-about-highly-sensitive-people/

Emotional management skills: what they are and how to develop them. (n.d.). Indeed Career Guide. https://www.indeed.com/career-advice/career-development/emotional-management-skills

Ewers, K. (2021, June 1). *Nutritional tips for the highly sensitive person (HSP).* Dr. Keesha. https://www.drkeesha.com/nutritional-tips-for-the-highly-sensitive-person-hsp/

59 phrases to help you set boundaries. (2021, August 23). PR Daily. https://www.prdaily.com/59-phrases-to-help-you-set-boundaries/

5 reasons why recognising your emotions is important. (n.d.). BBC Teach. https://www.bbc.co.uk/teach/five-reasons-why-recognising-emotions/z7gxjhv

Forleo, M. (n.d.). *"Sensitivity is a sign of strength. It's not about toughening up, it's about smartening up."* Quote Fancy. https://quotefancy.com/quote/1716073/Marie-Forleo-Sensitivity-is-a-sign-of-strength-Its-not-about-toughening-up-it-s-about

14 things highly sensitive people need for happiness. (n.d.). Psychology Today. https://www.psychologytoday.com/us/blog/the-secret-lives-introverts/201808/14-things-highly-sensitive-people-need-happiness

The good and bad of emotion regulation strategies. (2015). Psychology Today. https://www.psychologytoday.com/us/blog/between-you-and-me/201509/the-good-and-bad-emotion-regulation-strategies

Granneman, J. (2014, October 18). *14 advantages of being highly sensitive.* Introvert, Dear. https://introvertdear.com/news/highly-sensitive-person-advantages/

Granneman, J. (2015, January 29). *For highly sensitive people: True stories of empowerment.* Introvert, Dear. https://introvertdear.com/news/highly-sensitive-people-read-true-story-empowerment/

Granneman, J. (2019, December 13). *21 signs you're a highly sensitive person.* Highly Sensitive Refuge. https://highlysensitiverefuge.com/highly-sensitive-person-signs/

Hardman, J. (2021, July 6). *How to set boundaries as a highly sensitive person —with scripts!* Josephine Hardman, PhD. https://josephinehardman.com/how-to-set-boundaries-highly-sensitive-person-with-scripts/

Help me understand: Why am I so sensitive? (2021, October 11). Psych Central. https://psychcentral.com/health/why-am-i-so-sensitive#can-i-stop-being-so-sensitive

Highly sensitive child parenting strategies. (n.d.). Atlas Psychology. https://www.atlaspsychologycollective.com/blog/highly-sensitive-child-parenting-strategies

Highly sensitive person. (n.d.). Psychology Today. https://www.psycholo gytoday.com/us/basics/highly-sensitive-person

Highly sensitive person trait + characteristics. (n.d.). Expansive Heart Psychotherapy. https://www.expansiveheart.com/highly-sensitive-person

Highly sensitive person traits that create more stress. (n.d.). Verywell Mind. https://www.verywellmind.com/highly-sensitive-persons-traits-that-create-more-stress-4126393

Highly sensitive person: Signs, strengths, and challenges. (2022, February 11). Medical News Today. https://www.medicalnewstoday.com/articles/highly-sensitive-person#signs

How to control your emotions: 11 strategies to try. (2020, April 28). Healthline. https://www.healthline.com/health/how-to-control-your-emotions#get-some-space

How to deal with people who repeatedly violate your boundaries. (2016, July 11). Psych Central. https://psychcentral.com/blog/imperfect/2016/07/how-to-deal-with-people-who-repeatedly-violate-your-boundaries#First

How to improve your emotion regulation skills for better health. (n.d.). Verywell Mind. https://www.verywellmind.com/emotion-regulation-skills-training-425374

How to parent a sensitive child live in a less than sensitive world. (n.d.). Verywell Family. https://www.verywellfamily.com/parenting-a-sensitive-child-8-discipline-strategies-1094942

How to set healthy boundaries. (n.d.). Verywell Health. https://www.verywellhealth.com/setting-boundaries-5208802

The importance of boundaries. (n.d.). Glassman-Psyd. https://www.glassmanpsyd.com/the-importance-of-boundaries

The importance of managing emotions. (n.d.). Health Hub. https://www.healthhub.sg/programmes/186/MindSG/Caring-For-Ourselves/Managing-Our-Emotions-Adults

Ishler, J. (2021, August 18). *How to set boundaries as a highly sensitive person.* HelloGiggles. https://hellogiggles.com/lifestyle/health-fitness/highly-sensitive-person-boundaries/

Kassmeier, E. (2020, October 12). *3 benefits of knowing your strengths.* Zaengle. https://zaengle.com/blog/benefits-using-strengths-work

Killian, J. (2021, February 22). *8 ways to tell if you're a highly sensitive person.* Anxiety Therapist in New Haven. https://arcadiancounsel ing.com/8-ways-tell-youre-highly-sensitive-person

Levay, N. (2018, August 10). *Sensitive people and boundaries.* Specialized Therapy. https://www.specializedtherapy.com/highly-sensitive-people-and-empaths-boundaries/

Martin, S. (2021, August 6). *Boundaries for the highly sensitive person.* Live Well with Sharon Martin. https://www.livewellwithsharonmartin.com/boundaries-highly-sensitive-person/

Middlemarch quotes. (n.d.). GoodReads. https://www.goodreads.com/work/quotes/1461747-middlemarch

Mogahed, Y. (n.d.). *"Your beauty is in your sensitivity. Don't let anyone take it from you."* Quote Fancy. https://quotefancy.com/quote/941097/Yasmin-Mogahed-Your-beauty-is-in-your-sensitivity-Don-t-let-anyone-take-it-from-you

Pillay, H. (2014, March 24). *Why it's important to know your strengths and weaknesses.* Leaderonomics. https://www.leaderonomics.com/arti cles/personal/why-its-important-to-know-your-strengths-and-weaknesses

Saint, D. (n.d.). *"You cannot make everyone think and feel as deeply as you do. This is your tragedy, because you understand them but they do not understand you."* GoodReads. https://www.goodreads.com/quotes/7968125-you-cannot-make-everyone-think-and-feel-as-deeply-as

Sensory processing disorder: causes, symptoms, and treatment. (n.d.). WebMD. https://www.webmd.com/children/sensory-processing-disorder

Setting boundaries. (n.d.). WebMD. https://www.webmd.com/mental-health/setting-boundaries

7 effective tips for (high) sensitive persons to improve health and happiness. (n.d.). Ankewebersmit.com. https://ankewebersmit.com/7-diet-tips-hsp-health-happiness/

7 myths to stop believing about highly sensitive people. (n.d.). Bustle. https://

www.bustle.com/p/7-myths-to-stop-believing-about-highly-sensitive-people-9752736

7 types of boundaries you may need. (2020, April 23). Psych Central. https://psychcentral.com/blog/imperfect/2020/04/7-types-of-boundaries-you-may-need#5

6 types of boundaries & questions to explore them. (2021, March 8). Urban Wellness. https://urbanwellnesscounseling.com/6-types-of-boundaries/

Soghomonian, I. (2019, September 23). *Boundaries—Why are they important?* The Resilience Centre. https://www.theresiliencecentre.com.au/boundaries-why-are-they-important/

Stewart, L. (2019, May 6). *10 ways to care for a highly sensitive person.* Highly Sensitive Refuge. https://highlysensitiverefuge.com/care-for-a-highly-sensitive-person/

Stewart, L. (2021, February 26). *How HSPs can deal with negative emotions (and actually feel better).* Introvert, Dear. https://introvertdear.com/news/negative-emotions-highly-sensitive-person/

Taylor, A. (n.d.). *"Love yourself enough to set boundaries. Your time and energy are precious. You get to choose how you use it. You teach people how to treat you by choosing what you will and won't accept."* Sanvello. https://www.sanvello.com/community/quotes/post/5673988

10 ways to build and preserve better boundaries. (2021, June 3). Psych Central. https://psychcentral.com/lib/10-way-to-build-and-preserve-better-boundaries#others-boundaries

3 ways to set boundaries with people. (n.d.). WikiHow. https://www.wikihow.com/Set-Boundaries-with-People

Top 7 challenges of highly sensitive people, according to a therapist, The. (2020, October 7). Highly Sensitive Refuge. https://highlysensitiverefuge.com/top-7-challenges-of-highly-sensitive-people-according-to-a-therapist/

Top 10 survival tips for the highly sensitive person (HSP). (n.d.). Psychology Today. https://www.psychologytoday.com/us/blog/prescriptions-life/201105/top-10-survival-tips-the-highly-sensitive-person-hsp

The untold story of being a highly sensitive person (HSP). (2020, December

18). Milenio Stadium. https://mileniostadium.com/opiniao/sara-dias/the-untold-story-of-being-a-highly-sensitive-person-hsp/

What is a highly sensitive person? (A relatable guide). (n.d.). Highly Sensitive Refuge. https://highlysensitiverefuge.com/what-is-highly-sensitive-person/

Wilding, M. (2021, December 10). *3 ways highly sensitive people can tap into their unique superpower.* Fast Company. https://www.fastcompany.com/90704450/3-ways-highly-sensitive-people-can-tap-into-their-unique-superpower-to-their-advantage

Wilkinson, J. (2020, October 28). *The benefits of regulating your emotions.* Wellspace Counseling. https://www.wellspacepdx.com/post/the-benefits-of-regulating-your-emotions

Winchell, R. (n.d.). *10 ways to support the highly sensitive person in your life.* The Mighty. https://themighty.com/2016/10/how-to-support-a-highly-sensitive-loved-one/

Made in the USA
Middletown, DE
03 September 2023

37899568R00096